CUSTOMER IN THE BOARDROOM?

Rama Bijapurkar is one of India's most respected thought leaders on market strategy and consumer-related issues. She is also a keen commentator on social and cultural changes in liberalizing India.

She has, over the last twenty-two years of her independent consulting practice, worked with an impressive list of Indian and global companies, guiding the development of their business-market strategies. She describes her mission as bringing 'market focus and customer-centricity to business strategy'.

Rama is one of India's most experienced independent directors, having served on the boards of several of India's blue-chip companies, across sectors. Past and present boards include Infosys Technologies, CRISIL, Axis Bank, ICICI Bank, Godrej Consumer Products, Nestlé India, Sun Pharma, Cummins India, Arvind Mills, ICICI Prudential Life Insurance, Mahindra Holidays & Resorts India, Mahindra & Mahindra Financial Services, etc.

An alumna of the Indian Institute of Management Ahmedabad, Rama continues to be involved with her alma mater, where she has been a visiting faculty for three decades, served on its board of governors and is presently professor of management practice.

Rama's work experience has been in market research and strategy consulting and, prior to setting up her own practice, included senior positions with McKinsey & Company, MARG Marketing and Research Group (which later became AC Nielsen India) and Mode Services (which later became TNS India).

She is also the author of *We Are like That Only: Understanding the Logic of Consumer India* and *A Never-Before World: Understanding the Evolution of Consumer India*.

INDIA'S BESTSELLING BUSINESS BOOKS SERIES

IIM
AHMEDABAD
BUSINESS BOOKS

CUSTOMER IN THE BOARDROOM?

Crafting Customer-Based
Business Strategy

RAMA BIJAPURKAR

Rama Bijapurkar

PENGUIN
BUSINESS

An imprint of Penguin Random House

PENGUIN BUSINESS

USA | Canada | UK | Ireland | Australia
New Zealand | India | South Africa | China | Singapore

Penguin Business is part of the Penguin Random House group of companies
whose addresses can be found at global.penguinrandomhouse.com

Published by Penguin Random House India Pvt. Ltd
4th Floor, Capital Tower 1, MG Road,
Gurugram 122 002, Haryana, India

First published by Sage Publications Ltd 2012
Published in Penguin Business by Penguin Random House India 2023

Copyright © Rama Bijapurkar 2012

10 9 8 7 6 5 4 3 2

The views and opinions expressed in this book are the author's own and the
facts are as reported by her which have been verified to the extent possible,
and the publishers are not in any way liable for the same.

ISBN 9780143461302

Typeset in Sabon by Manipal Technologies Limited, Manipal

Printed at Repro India Limited

www.penguin.co.in

This is a legitimate digitally printed version of the book and therefore might not
have certain extra finishing on the cover.

This book owes its existence to:
My clients, from whom I have learnt so much
over the years.
My students, who have made me
repeatedly rethink what
I thought I knew.
Abhinandan Jain, my teacher and thought partner,
co-creator and co-instructor of our
Customer-Based Business Strategy course at IIMA.

Contents

Contents

Preface and Acknowledgements

I spent a large part of my mid-career years searching for the Holy Grail of my work, which I finally conceptualized as follows:

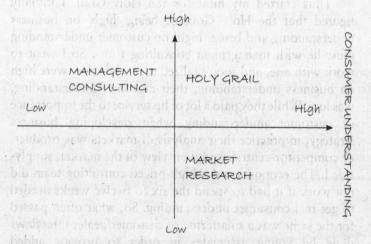

My professional journey began in market research, where I spent almost two decades. Sometime in the middle of that sojourn, the realization dawned on me that while we were doing a great job of consumer/ customer understanding (whichever way the customer was defined), our understanding of our clients' business imperatives was very limited.

As a result, even though we were dealing with companies whose business end games/strategic intents were quite different from each other, as were their core competencies and sources of competitive advantage, our market research approach remained the same for all of them. We would research the market and obtain customer understanding in exactly the *same way* for a champion and a challenger business, for an MNC with a fixed global strategy and a local company with great strategic flexibility, and so on. I was uncomfortable with the quality of strategic decision support that our work was providing to our clients.

Thus started my hunt for the Holy Grail. I initially figured that the Holy Grail of being 'high' on business understanding and being 'high' on customer understanding must lie with management consulting firms. So I went to work with one, and soon realized that while they were high on business understanding, their customer understanding, was low. While they paid a lot of lip service to the importance of customer understanding when developing business strategy, in practice their analysis of markets was product- or competitor-centric, and their view of the market, supply-sided. The economics of a high-priced consulting team did not work if it had to spend the six to twelve weeks needed to get real consumer understanding. So, what often passed for the same was a smattering of customer/dealer interviews done by young associates in order to provide added flavour to the industry-analysis-based business strategy recommendations.

I did, however, learn two very important things from my brief stint at the management consulting firm which brought me closer to my Holy Grail—one was to apply theoretical business strategy development frameworks to real-life business situations, and the other was to model the long-term financial implications of marketing strategy recommendations that glibly rolled out of the marketing mouth. As I wondered what to do next, I was given some very sage advice by Dr Indira Parikh, the then dean of IIM Ahmedabad. She said that if there was a game I desperately wanted to play, that only I knew how to play, then I had no option other than to create my own playground and my own rules and persuade others to play it with me. That's how I set up my own consulting practice a dozen years ago—to play my dream game of consulting on customer-based business strategy.

Along the way, about eight years ago, along with Abhinandan Jain (professor, IIM-A), we created a course named Customer-Based Business Strategy (CBBS). The purpose of this was to spread the gospel, of course, but also to force ourselves to capture and codify our learning from consulting. The slightly wicked part of it, though, was that we wanted to design a course that could compete, in the strategy area, directly with the prevalent popular strategy course CCCS—Core Competence and Competitive Strategy. We thought that CCCS was the ultimate 'inside-out and supply-side' view of developing business strategy and CBBS was exactly the opposite 'outside-in' way of doing the same!

Every journey begins with a single step and is enriched, along the way, with contributions from many others. We too had a lot of people who joined us in our voyage, and we will be forever grateful to them. We started with a half credit course and want to thank Dr A.S. Ganguly (former chairman of Hindustan Lever and Director Unilever PLC, presently member, Rajya Sabha) for being the first visitor to come and talk to our class and encourage us to go forth in our endeavour.

Since then, we have tried hard to get the CEO practitioner/strategy developer's voice into our course and want to thank all those who spared the time and effort to come and share their experiences freely. Arun Adhikari (now Chairman, Unilever, Japan) was an early and regular visiting faculty, as have been Bhaskar Bhatt (MD, Titan) and Jerry Rao (former chairman, Mphasis). Deepak Satwalekar (then MD, HDFC Standard Life Insurance), Roopa Kudva (MD, Crisil), Ireena Vittal (partner, McKinsey & Company), Gopal Vittal (director, Hindustan Unilever), Atul Sobti (then MD, Hero Honda), Sanjay Purohit (head of corporate planning, Infosys), Prashant Pande (MD, Radio Mirchi), Ravi Rajagopalan (entrepreneur in the mobile payments space) and Madhivanan Balakrishnan (executive director, ICICI Prulife Insurance) are people we want to thank for making our CBBS course closer to the real world. We also tested and worked on our ideas by running several two- to four-day management development programmes with practicing managers.

My consulting practice has been squarely in this area, and I have learnt a lot from the clients I have worked with and even more from all my colleagues on the many boards that I have served on. In addition, Tino Puri (former director McKinsey & Company) deserves a special mention for his repeated and dazzling demonstrations of the difference between the religion of strategy and the rituals that most strategy developers focus on. S. Ramchander, who sadly is not with us anymore, spent several long hours over the years sharing ideas and helping push the envelope further. C. K. Prahalad, my teacher at IIMA, and mentor since, lives on in all the work that I do, and this book is no exception.

Thank you Sugata (Sugata Ghosh, Sage Publications) for the patience, the good-humoured high-intensity arguments and the hard work in both shaping the book and in saving me from myself!

My mother's dining table is where my books have their critical rites of passage, and this one has been similarly blessed.

Last, but never ever the least, thank you Lucy for taking charge of the book from the stage of the untidy scrawls, written in twenty-minute stretches at airport lounges and sleepy late nights, to keeping track of a zillion versions in shoddily labelled electronic files, and for helping me plough through mounds of edit queries. And what can I say to you, Ashoke? Thank you for suggesting the title, for critically reading the book at every stage and for never once grumbling about the untidy heaps of paper and reference books perennially occupying half the dining table at home.

Aparna, I hope you will approve of this effort of your mom. Surely, it will be not that much more boring than those economics books you read with admiration?

Prologue

WHY BOTHER WITH STRATEGY IN A HYPER GROWTH ENVIRONMENT

Looking back at the last decade, it is clear that India Inc.'s thinking about business strategy has been shaped by the environment of hyper growth that it has operated in, and been driven by the relentless growth-worshipping business valuation regime. In fact, since 1991, India Inc. has witnessed significant and steady sales growths as a result of increases in consumption of one billion people getting richer—or becoming less poor—and feeling more secure and confident about spending. Consequently, the demand side of business has never really been an area of strategic focus, and in a land of abundance, nobody lost much sleep worrying about the quality and nature of custom that a business had.

India Inc. has, therefore, operated with the implicit logic that 'if you expand supply and manage operations well, you will win big time', and focused on building efficient supply machines that were capable of making maximum hay while the sun shone. If making choices is at the heart of strategy, India Inc. had no time for that—why choose what kind of fish you want when the tumultuous tide is sweeping in all kinds of fish into a one-size-fits-all net? The success of this approach is evident from revenue and profit growth over the past decade and a half.

Even though the demand side of the market has never been a real cause for concern, it has been a source of discomfort several times since 1991. There have been many blips, off and on, of slowing demand; some were caused by a few scattered years of low economic growth as a result of environmental shocks, but the economy proved to be resilient and amply made up for them in subsequent years. Some of the demand problems were caused by misplaced bets on whether rural India or urban India would grow faster, whether the 'class market' would expand or the 'mass market' would explode earlier, and so on.

The most memorable blip was in the late 1990s when there was unwarranted optimism—animal spirits took precedence over income analysis— about the great Indian middle class, resulting in overinvestment in capacity. However, a few years later, all was well again, as demand caught up with or even surpassed supply. In response to these blips, India Inc. has learnt to switch effortlessly between two modes—one of fast and furious top line growth with some amount of careless bloating, during the good times; and the other, during the bad times, of ruthless and smart cost-cutting to make the supply machine leaner, meaner and fitter for the good times to come.

Looking ahead, there is every indication that this environment of hyper growth will continue—especially since India has successfully weathered the global downturn of 2008, with just one slow year in 2008–09, which still produced a respectable GDP growth of 6.5 per cent. The Indian economy is now firmly back on the growth trajectory. The usual popular sources of forecasting GDP growth such as international monetary fund (IMF), Morgan Stanley, economist intelligence unit (EIU), United Nations (UN), planning commission, etc., suggest that

India's GDP is expected to grow by about 7.5 per cent to 8 per cent in 2009–10, accelerating to over 8.5 per cent in the year after, and crossing 9 per cent from then on, if nothing goes gravely wrong. As a result of this, India's consumption story will continue to be awesome: from its current estimated GDP in 2011 of around USD 1.7 trillion, another USD 1.7 trillion or more of GDP will be added in the next seven to ten years, thereby doubling the size of India's economy.

Consequently, the country's population of over one billion people will, on average, nearly double its per capita income in the next decade, or even sooner than that. This, combined with the huge consumer and consumption confidence of Indian consumers based on the upward mobility they have experienced in the past decade and their keen desire to improve their quality of life and launch their children into a higher orbit of living, makes India truly a market where the tide will continuously rise. Between 2007 and 2025, according to a McKinsey study, 'The Bird of gold: The Rise of India's Consumer market' (2007), India's total consumption will quadruple, making India the fifth largest consumer market in the world by 2025.

The question is, will the prevalent approaches to business strategy, especially the low priority accorded to market strategy, i.e., strategizing the demand side of the business, work in the future too? We believe not. We believe that while consumption growth continues, there are far greater consumer and competition challenges that the next decade will bring; the old strategic mindset of 'it's just the supply side, stupid' may be enough to generate a healthy top and bottom line growth, but will not be enough to capture the high value opportunities of the future and build strong and hard-to-dislodge businesses.

Thus far, market strategy has been understood to be synonymous with aggression—considered to be the only useful weapon that ensures victory in the market. It is true that, in the last decade, fortune has indeed favoured the brave and the adventurous and has handsomely rewarded those who took the risks of venturing into new business lines and new geographies early. Bharti Telecom (Airtel) and ICICI are big, obvious and iconic examples of this era.

In the past decade, the dominant and favourite market strategies of India Inc. have been: 'Star Track' for the brave and the confident; 'Carpet Bomb' for the fast follower; and 'Sales Force' (pun intended) and 'Brand Shout'—both if you were especially frenzied or just one if you were a bit calmer.

The 'Star Track' market strategy is all about relentlessly pushing the existing business arena outwards and going where no one else has gone before and doing what you have not done before, be it in terms of new geographies, new services and products, or new avenues of distribution. The 'Star Track' strategy is based on the logic that whoever gets there first (the first mover) will be the winner and will remain so for all times to come, leaving only the crumbs for all those who came later. However, it is now clear that a first mover advantage is sustainable only if you get there first *and* lock up something that the next guy cannot have. Otherwise, the next guy and the next will inevitably get there, often learning from the pioneer's mistakes. Eventually, as in the case of banks and telecom companies, everyone looks the same—the same suite of products, the same service paradigms, the same execution efficiencies (give or take some at the margin), the same pricing and the same geographic spread and distribution.

The 'Carpet Bombing' market strategy is based on the belief that proliferation is the key to market success.

While Star Track warriors constantly go to new frontiers, Carpet Bombers stay in the space they are in, but proliferate everything—products, services, alliances and activities. '20 × 20' is a typical 'strategy slogan' of this type of business—20 products in 20 months (think two-wheelers, liquor and soaps) or 20 alliances in 20 countries or 20 arenas (think pharmaceuticals and chemicals). It is all about 'ready–fire–aim' in the hope that by the laws of large numbers, at least one of them would hit a lucrative target. In a crowded market, such proliferation is already leading to higher costs of complexity, spreading resources thin, confusing customers into commodity type buying behaviour and leading to diminishing returns.

The 'Sales Force' market strategy, the most inward looking of them all, is based on the belief that there is no such thing as a real competitive advantage and that muscle is everything. This approach mirrors the military tactic of 'shock and awe', which is based on the use of overwhelming power and spectacular displays of force. Practitioners of Sales Force talk of their business as being a 'push' and not a 'pull' business, and their motto is 'push–push–push'. Therefore, if hit rates of contacts to sales are very low, then instead of examining the consumer reasons for low conversion and consumer-oriented remedies for increasing hit rates, their response is to increase the contact base. As businesses grow, the incremental effort needed to maintain a decent revenue growth rate using Sales Force requires huge armies of 'feet on the street' and reaches herculean proportions, often unsustainable.

The 'Brand Shout' aficionados thrive on the belief that brand recall and visibility is everything, and think of brand promotion as some form of voodoo magic which will make customers flock to them. They shout louder, are more visible, sponsor every event in sight and get a galaxy of celebrities to endorse their products or businesses. With each celebrity now endorsing several unrelated products, the customer is now a healthy sceptic, and the celebrity the only one laughing all the way to the bank. Besides, in hard times, the first plug that India Inc. pulls is that of advertising and brand investment, leading to really patchy brand building. The bigger problem, though, is that in the absence of a real market strategy driving the brand communication effort, many brands are just well recognized trademarks, rather than names that trigger associations and values in the minds of the customers.

However, the demand side is not going to be as easy to manage in the future with such tactical and operational market 'strategies'. Some of the changed characteristics in the demand environment of the future will be:

- For a start, even nowadays, there are a lot more things for people to buy, and income growths are not large enough to accommodate all of them. This phenomenon will continue in the foreseeable future. The competition for the consumer rupee will be severe. and the consumer will not allocate his money at the level of categories and then search for brands within these categories. Rather, the competition for the wallet will be cut across categories and be between eating out at the new restaurant 'China Express' versus a movie at Inox theatre versus a higher EMI on a housing loan to buy a bigger-than-necessary house going at a bargain price versus a package tour to Rome.
- Second, there is increasing competition in every sector and multiple competitive strategies to deal with. The numbers 2, 3, and 4 in each market have now grown big

enough to pose real challenges to market leaders. The other phenomenon is also working—there are too many me-too competitors, all fighting on price and destroying value in most categories, forcing the big boys with higher cost bases to differentiate themselves or bleed. A market strategy that fights on both fronts is the key to survival.

- Third, there is the problem of plenty that is facing companies—plenty of consumers as well as plenty of competitors. It is a mixed blessing to have such rapid consumption growth because it means more heterogeneous customer segments and more diverse product requirements. More players in a sector, especially some with deep pockets and longer-term perspectives, means many more new products, new distribution strategies, and frequent price wars to deal with. Responding to each competitor's move is getting increasingly complex and is leading to diffused focus and risking the existing successful business. Companies are realizing that they need to define their own way of playing to win in the market and to hold their own course despite competitive shenanigans in the market.

- Finally, winning through increases in operational efficiency is going to get increasingly harder and less profitable. Michael Porter, in an article in *Harvard Business Review* (November–December 1996) titled 'What Is Strategy', makes the point that 'operational effectiveness is not strategy'. He concedes that operational effectiveness was 'at the heart of the Japanese challenge to Western companies in the 1980s'. However he goes on to say:

. . . imagine for a moment a *productivity frontier* that constitutes the sum of all existing best practices at any given time. Think of it as the maximum value that a company delivering a particular product or service can create at a given cost, using the best available technologies, skills, management techniques, and purchased inputs. . . . When a company improves its operational effectiveness, it moves towards the [productivity] frontier. Doing so may require capital investment, different personnel or simply new ways of managing.

The productivity frontier is constantly shifting outwards as new technologies and management approaches are developed, and as new inputs become available . . . OE [operational effectiveness] competition shifts the productivity frontier outward, effectively raising the bar for everyone. But although such competition produces absolute improvements in operational effectiveness, it leads to relative improvement for no one. . . . the resulting major productivity gains are being captured by customers and suppliers [but] not retained in superior profitability.

Supply-focused business strategies may still hold good for another three to five years, but they will produce diminishing returns. However, trying to respond, continuously and tactically, to competition moves in the market or to environmental opportunities or threats, without a strong customer-centric strategic compass, will be more confusing and more exhausting. and then, there will come a time, not too far away, when the stock market and private investors will reward those who have not just delivered good numbers year on year, but have a strong and differentiated market position which de-risks the business. In fact, recent equity analysts reports and questions being asked by late stage private equity investors, suggest that there is now far greater interest and concern than earlier about the quality of the business engine rather than just about the speed that it is running at. Investors are probing much more into the quality of growth, its sustainability and whether the systems and processes, structures and governance models and the people power to manage growth are well in place. If it is a choice between a short-sprint champion with no evidence of ability to manage and sustain growth and a slow-but-steady marathon runner with a clear future plan, the preference could well be for the latter even among medium-term investors.

Clearly, it is time for India Inc. to open a new chapter of business strategy, which looks beyond how to capture a bigger share of industry growth by building a lean, mean supply machine that fires on all cylinders, and makes market strategy the centrepiece of business strategy, thinking seriously about what games the company will play in the market and why and how, as:

> That is what this book is about. It discusses ways and means to bring market and customer focus to business strategy, thus enabling companies to build sustainable market positions. It promotes an understanding of how to read markets in order to shape business direction, and learning how to create wealth for the business by adding value to the customer.

CHAPTER 1

Introduction

When we tell businesspeople that the course we teach at the Indian Institute of Management (IIM) Ahmedabad is called Customer-Based Business Strategy (CBBS), we often get the puzzled response: 'But is there any other kind of strategy?' Obviously there is, because if we apply a simple test of how early in the business strategy document of companies the word *customer* (not *market*) first appears, the business strategies of most companies would fare very badly.

THE WALK–TALK GAP IN CUSTOMER-CENTRICITY

A customer-centric approach usually remains confined to the realm of the downstream operational activities of most companies, as is evident from the typical actions that they take to become more customer-centric. For example, they routinely restructure the sales organization and re-designate sales executives as *customer care* executives as the primary way to gain more traction with customers. In some companies, metrics relating to customer-centricity are included in the key result areas (KRAs) of the senior management. However, at the time of performance appraisals, judgements are usually based on sales data or on the current levels of customer satisfaction or loyalty, which again are in the domain of the marketing manager's business operations and not in the domain of the CEO's formulation of business strategy. We know of business groups that give great weightage to the Net Promoter Score (NPS) of each of their businesses in order to determine the CEO's bonus. (NPS is a measure of how loyal the customers are—for more details refer to Note 1.) However, a high NPS is possible even when a business serves a small segment of the market, and the CEO does not get penalized for a blinkered business strategy that ignores huge opportunities in emerging customer segments. Therefore, 'customer-centricity' metrics even at the CEO level do not usually measure the extent of customer-centricity in developing the business strategy of the company. Further, with the increasing adoption of the balanced score card to monitor business health and measure the performance of business strategy beyond mere financials—on dimensions of *customer*, *learning* and *processes*—we would have expected the more strategic metrics of customer-centricity that are more relevant to business strategy (such as a shift in the customer segment mix or an improvement in customer-perceived advantage over competition on dimension 'X' or 'Y' or percentage of business turnover or profit that came on account of new customers attracted, because of new models of payment, etc.).

However, the metrics typically used for even the *customer* section of the balanced score card are *financial* metrics restated to appear like customer metrics (for example, value of sales from top 10 customers), or they are generic operational metrics like customer satisfaction or loyalty, or worse still, the high-level catch-all metric of market share.

Consequently, the efforts that companies make to achieve customer-centricity are, as we said earlier, in the realm of improving downstream operations, and not in the realm of improving the quality of strategy. They are squarely in the realm of *executing* or implementing the already chosen business strategy in the marketplace.

CUSTOMER-CENTRICITY MUST BE EMBEDDED INTO BUSINESS STRATEGY

Modern business strategy theorists the world over are increasingly advocating that customer-centricity must be present right at the stage of the *creation* or *development* of a business strategy. This is best summed up in the title of a recent highly successful book on business strategy, *Blue Ocean Strategy: How to Create Uncontested Market Space and Make Competition Irrelevant* (Kim and Mauborgne, 2005). Kenichi Ohmae, strategy guru and author of *The Borderless World: Power and Strategy in the Interlinked Economy* (1999) and *The Mind of the Strategist: The Art of Japanese Business* (1991), made the same point in a hallmark article in the *Harvard Business Review* in 1988, titled 'Getting Back to Strategy', and said that in today's competitive environment, strategy means paying 'painstaking attention' to customers' needs, 'rethinking' what your product is, what it does and how you 'design, build, and market it'.

In essence, business strategies themselves, and not merely their implementation, must be customer-centric or, as we term it, *customer-based* or customer-driven!

We often need to remind our CEO clients about the direct linkage between customers' desires and behaviour and the financials (top line and cost line, and hence profit) of a company.

The *top line* or the revenue line of the profit and loss (P&L) statement is not the result of the company getting 'x' per cent share of a given market. Rather, the market share the company gets is the result of the revenue it earns. The top line of a P&L statement is directly linked to how many customers buy a company's product or service, at what price they buy, how often they buy and what quantity they buy each time.

The *cost line* of a company's P&L is also linked to customers. It is determined by:

1. What it costs to actually produce things that customers want to buy,
2. What it costs to get the product to the place the customers want to buy from and
3. What it costs the company to supervise this entire operation.

The *profit*—or *loss*—is merely the resultant number of revenue minus costs, that is, of this entire process of how the company engages with its customers or consumers. (The word 'consumer' is usually used by business-to-consumer [B2C] businesses, and the word 'customer' in business-to-business [B2B] businesses. B2C businesses usually refer to their dealers and distributors as customers, and their end users as consumers. Since we believe that the concepts discussed in this book are equally relevant to both B2B and B2C businesses, in this book, we use the two words interchangeably throughout this book.)

We also frequently remind CEOs that business goals eventually require customer/consumer cooperation if they are to be achieved. For example, strategic moves, such as mergers and acquisitions, which are aimed at achieving

4

revenue growth, are all about the hope of value creation as a result of the increased customer base, or the increase in the ability of the company as a whole to better serve a wider variety of customers and hence be the preferred option to a much greater extent than either of the companies alone. Even business diversification decisions are about companies wanting to access a greater share of the customers' expenditure.

'Competitive strategy' too is not merely about competitors—it is about making customers believe that you are better than the competition! Business objectives like 'achieve growth', 'improve market position' (market share, market perception), or 'improve margins' are all about acquiring new customers, getting existing ones to buy at a higher price performance point or buy more from one company and less of the other. Ultimately, all business strategy objectives are usually ultimately related to growing/ maintaining revenue and/or profit and decreasing costs and sustaining it year after year. Generically speaking, this requires, as we have discussed earlier, getting certain types of customers to behave in a particular manner that benefits the company. It, therefore, stands to reason that the business strategy for achieving these business objectives must be built around consumers and customers too.

However, in practice, the customer usually gets left out of the process of the development of a business strategy. *Market analysis* does form a key element of the basis on which business strategy is developed, but the market is thought of as the sum total of *industry sales* and not as the total of *consumer spends*. Therefore, much of business strategy development is unimaginatively, and even dangerously, based on how the market is defined—typically it is defined by the sales of a set of *peer group companies*.

For example, a company manufacturing 150 cc motorcycles would develop its business strategy on the basis of a market defined as equal to the sales of two-wheelers and not as the expenditure on transportation by a certain kind of customer or consumer. Worse still, the market may get defined even more narrowly as sales of motorcycles, or, even worse, of 150 cc motorcycles. Most business strategy development processes do not work the notion that markets are made of the money that people spend to fulfil a need or want and not the sales of companies that sell a certain widget. This leads to the formulation of very suboptimal business strategies.

THE DEMAND-SIDED VIEW IS OFTEN IGNORED

We find that even the most self-proclaimed customer-centric companies often adopt a totally supply-sided view of the business when developing their business strategy. They do, however, feel that they are being market-focused because they think about their strategy in terms of geographies and competition, but the fact is that they do not factor the customer or consumer into their analysis. This leads to business strategy being defined in the following ways:

- Either in 'inside–out' terms such as 'grow inorganically by acquiring company X', 'reorganize supply chain to reduce total inventory in the system', 'move product mix towards higher margin products/services', or 'improve operating margin by 3 per cent by focusing on five areas of improvement';
- In terms of competition such as 'target PQR product segments where competition is weak and increase market share'; or

6

- Mostly, in concession to the market out there, defined in terms of geographic and/or product range completion such as 'aggressively expand to class B and C towns with low price range', 'enter three adjacent businesses and become an integrated supplier', or 'launch the following five products so as to compete in all segments of the market'.

What is clearly absent in these strategies is thinking related to how consumer behaviour can be changed by adopting a different business model (for example, pay as you use, or not use regularly, but for specific occasions), or targeting new consumers' needs or migrating the business to serve new types of customer groups, or doing something to gain a larger share of consumer wallets or consumer spend in parts of the value chain that the business is not playing in, and so on. 'But should such types of questions really be a part of business strategy?' we are sometimes asked. We believe they most certainly should, because they constitute paths to achieve business goals—and that is what business strategy is all about. As we have discussed earlier, the financial performance of a business is the result of consumer behaviour. Hence, even a business goal such as 'improve operating margin' or 'improve gross margin on XYZ product line' requires customer-centricity. The full problem statement would be: 'How to find ways to ensure that cost-cutting does not impact future growth or impair the health and value of the business?', that is, how to ensure that the actions we take internally do not turn off future customers, decrease the consumption of existing customers, make them re-evaluate the perceived value of a cheaper and less-beneficial competitive product, or switch to a higher-priced alternative means of doing something that eliminates the usage of the present products altogether (buy an electric grill because the Teflon coating on the non-stick pan does not last as long as it used to). Customer behaviour and attitude change goals are part of business strategy because they contribute to ways in which revenue and profit objectives can be met.

It is also true that business strategy deals with complex issues like restructuring business portfolios or financial restructuring of businesses. Does customer-centricity play a role in these? Yes, it does. In our experience, it is not uncommon to find businesses that look like 'dogs' when viewed from the supply-side lens, but are actually 'stars' when viewed from the customer lens. In the case of corporate portfolio restructuring, the basis on which businesses are retained, put on the block or are heavily invested in, is almost always determined by an analysis what is happening in the so-called 'market' (that is, industry/competitor/regulator). However, taking the consumer into account in this analysis could lead to different decisions that could create more value for the company. To illustrate this with an example of the consumer durables retail business in India: From a conventional supply-sided 'industry' view, and a 'market (excluding customer)' view, this would not be seen as a good business to retain because the *industry* rate of growth is slowing down, while competition in this space is about to increase sharply, and the overall industry margins in this business have not been great. However, if the decision were to be based on the view from the customer world, this business would be a star business and not a dog or a question-mark business.

The study of the business through the lens of consumers would tell a totally different story—one of low-hanging fruit or unrealized potential waiting to be tapped: There is no pan-Indian consumer durables retail chain to serve a customer base that is getting richer and gadgetizing their lives rapidly. Upper–upper-income homes have a host of reasonably old durables that they would be ready to upgrade to state-of-the-art new models if only someone energized them to do so, such as getting a flat screen in place of a regular colour TV or a clothes drier to accompany the washing machine. These homes or consumers also have several latent needs that can easily be brought to the surface, like a hands-free attachment for the mobile phone on the steering wheel of a car. Further, the fact that more households have both the husband and the wife leading busy lives and spending a lot of time outside the house provides an interesting revenue-generating opportunity to lock in customers for a lifetime through service. As for the competition, the question to examine is not the supply-side question of how many competitors there are in the market, but the consumer-centric question of whether the competitors have any special advantages that the customer appreciates and which will be hard to beat. If not, then the mere fact that more competitors are entering the market should not be a cause for worry.

Let us look at another example. How do companies counter declining sales or severe competition eroding their market share? A typical example is that of a company we knew in the chemicals business. When ships from China started arriving with similar quality products at far lower prices, the CEO's response was to invite us to conduct a workshop with the sales team to teach them how to sell more forcefully. He also felt that bolstering the brand using some advertising and PR could help. However, what he was not facing up to was the fact that this decline in sales was not an operating marketing performance issue. It was an issue of a fundamentally uncompetitive business that needed to be dealt with at the business strategy level. The business needed to ask: Who (customer types) is out there who would be willing to pay higher prices for some benefit that he would appreciate, how should the company gear itself to offer that benefit profitably? The answer could lie in better and cheaper transportation of the chemical to the factory, better inventory management done for the customer, just-in-time deliveries or flexible shipping schedules, and so on.

Another situation where business strategy developed with a demand-sided view produced different answers compared to conventionally developed business strategy was that of a tyre manufacturer whose revenue mostly came from replacement sales of truck tyres. He absolutely wanted to grow despite there being a recession in the economy. The only trouble was that there was not enough wear and tear on truck tyres since the transport business was down, and therefore, so was the need to replace tyres. In this situation teaching the sales force to sell smarter was not going to help. Neither would smarter advertising or pushing dealers, especially since the company was the market leader in the replacement truck tyre business and could not grow easily by grabbing market share from others. The answer to achieving the business growth objectives he had set for the next few years lay in finding different product–market customers to serve. Selling to Original Equipment Manufacturers (OEMs) of trucks was not worthwhile since OEMs were under a huge pricing pressure themselves and were squeezing suppliers. Making tyres for the passenger car market was an option because when it came to replacing tyres, car owners preferred to stick to the same brand that the car manufacturers (OEMs) had used. Hence, in order to play in the replacement car tyre market, selling to the unprofitable OEMs was unavoidable. Therefore, the company needed to search for some segment of tyre-buying customers who could be a source of profitable growth, given the company's capabilities in tyres. The answer did not come easily and involved a detailed mapping of truck owners and their tyre-buying behaviour. This yielded a large group of truckers who were buying retreaded tyres from small retreading shops, at prices well below that of new tyres, and who were concerned about the quality they were buying and the risks involved. Would it be possible for this company to partner with these small retreading shops and offer them better base 'bald' tyres and lock them in with credit? Could they then get a marginally higher price from their customers for better quality tyres? What sort of business model would this require and how could profitability be maximized? Thus, such business strategy questions often start with questions of how to get more customers or how to get the existing ones to stay and end up requiring fundamental changes in the business design itself.

IT IS VERY RISKY NOT TO BE CUSTOMER BASED IN THE FLUID WORLD OF EMERGING MARKETS

Beyond the usual well-known arguments of 'customer-centricity is good, is God', we would like to discuss the context of emerging markets to explain why we are such strong advocates of CBBS.

The world of emerging markets is in a state of flux. And it would be very risky not to be customer-based in such important markets of the future. Both suppliers and customers are rapidly evolving; notions of industry structure or even market size or business segments are yet to be frozen or set because the definition of an industry or even a product market is being continuously changed by the environment and competition; and the rules of the market are still being made and the winners are yet to be declared.

In such a situation, developing business strategy based on supply-side variables like the size and growth of market, existing product and price segments and competitors, and their strategies is dangerous. All of these will change as cost structures change, as the full suite of competitors enter the market disrupting existing price–performance equations and as customers are introduced to never-before products. Further, competitors are not always logical or rational in their actions, ready to lose significant amounts of money in order to build a sizeable market share that gives them clout with distribution channels. Clearly, a strategy based on 'where in the industry do you want to position yourself' and what generic strategy is appropriate for this industry configuration' is rather pointless.

Hence, in this scenario, implementing the classical ideas of competitive strategy is far tougher than starting from zero-base—from customer-based strategy.

The emerging market winners will be those who shape consumers and markets and gain competitive advantage by doing so—and shaping markets requires a deep understanding of how to get consumers to adopt totally new behaviour patterns that are advantageous to both the company and the consumers, but disadvantageous to competitors. Therefore, instead of looking at, for example, the Structure–Conduct–Performance-type classical industry analysis, we believe that looking at Consumer Demand Structure– Customer Conduct–Consumer Needs and levels of satisfaction with the options available will yield a far more robust business strategy.

WHY DOES CUSTOMER-CENTRICITY GET IGNORED?

Most companies' CEOs and strategists will have no difficulty agreeing with the discussion so far. Why, then, does customer-centricity not get its rightful place when business strategy is being developed? Despite having faith and desire for customer-centricity, why do companies not successfully incorporate it in their business strategy? Why do they restrict it to downstream operational marketing activities? The reason for this can largely be attributed to the way the marketing (or customer-consumer centricity) discipline has evolved and the way it has failed to get its place at the high table where strategy is developed.

A lot of literature in academic journals has discussed this (see McGovern et al. 2004; Ohmae 1988; Wind and Robertson 1983). The consensus seems to be that people who know and practise the marketing discipline (who understand customers better and know how to utilize that understanding for business gain) are very far removed from the place where business strategy is discussed. As McGovern et al. (2004) of the Harvard Business School say: 'When marketing activities are tightly aligned with corporate strategy, they drive growth. But in too many companies, marketing is poorly linked to strategy. In many organizations, marketing exists far from the executive suite and boardroom.' The converse is also true. It is common for business strategy developers to discuss business strategy in terms of every aspect of running a business except in terms of consumers or customers. Ironically, a lot of the great strategy books (see Kim and Mauborgne 2005; Hamel and Prahalad 1996) are full of consumer-related speak. But the truth is that there is no one in the strategy development

13

room who really thinks and acts with consumers or customers for a living. The CMO is just beginning to appear on the scene alongside the CFO to provide the perspective from the consumer angle. However, McGovern et al. (2004) suggest that instead of *bringing in* the customers' perspective, this phenomenon could actually be *taking it away* from boardrooms since the CMO is being delegated whatever little customer marketing thinking the CEO was doing thus far. (See Appendix 1 for a detailed description of the evolution of business strategy thinking and of the thinking of the role that marketing can play.)

For those still confused about why marketing must be mixed up with business strategy, we direct them to the source that has inspired our thinking—a special issue of the *Journal of Marketing* (Wind and Robertson, 1983) on marketing strategy, where marketing management was defined as 'addressing issue at the level of the individual product or brand', and as being 'most fundamentally concerned about the design of the marketing program or mix'. Marketing strategy, in contrast, was delineated as 'focusing explicitly on the quest for long run consumer, a competitive advantage for the firm or SBU as a whole'. Thus, the similarity, indeed synonymity, between business strategy and marketing strategy, both being concerned with the quest for long-run competitive advantage, was conceded. This perspective, when integrated with other perspectives such as finance, technology, human resources, etc., would form the basis for a holistic business strategy.

THIS BOOK . . .

This book was first published in 2012 and has been used as an anchor textbook for our MBA course for over two decades. Obviously, a lot has changed in the world of business, and equally obviously, a lot has not. In fact, there has never been a greater need for customer-centred business strategy in the rapidly changing world of blurring industry boundaries, frequent market disruption, especially by new-economy 'digital-first' companies, a plethora of fast followers for any innovation and the turbulence people (customers) are experiencing in their lives.

We talk to our students, a lot, about the twin ideas of conceptual clarity and context familiarity, emphasizing the distinction and highlighting the need for them to be on top of both. In my continuing journey across the boardrooms of India Inc., I am convinced that this book continues to be extremely relevant in terms of conceptual clarity and the examples provided are good, classical illustrations of concepts. Like all classics, they still offer value even though dated in time. Educators who use this book as resource material for their teaching need to augment it, as we do in our teaching, with newer examples and draw connections between some of the relabelled discourse on business strategy and these core concepts.

The objective of this book is to suggest a business strategy development *approach/framework/process* that enables business strategy to be rooted firmly in the world of consumers and to be designed to achieve the company's objectives and goals through having a certain *impact* in that world. The subsequent chapters cover the following ideas/concepts and provide a set of *how to* tools for implementing these:

1. A perspective on what business strategy is and where and how market analysis and consumer insight fit into the business strategy development processes that are usually followed.

2. The idea and concept of a business-market strategy: How it is different from a functional marketing strategy and how it is the *front end* of business strategy. The relationship between business-market strategy and a business strategy.

3. The concept of customer-based business-market segmentation for deciding the strategic market priorities of a business unit (that is, which parts of the market the business will play in and how hard): Today, market prioritization, for the purposes of business strategy, is done at the level of products or product markets or price slabs (for example, the 150 cc scooter segment we will develop/boilers for shipbuilding we will play in opportunistically/the premium price segment is where we will focus efforts, etc). We discuss how business-market segmentation can be done by using more customer-based variables for determining the strategic priorities of a company (for example, identifying long-distance commuters who would be the focus of the R&D of vehicle building or adopting a focused *mission* towards critical users of power like BPOs or progressive SMEs who are growth oriented, etc.). What is the advantage of this? Why does it make for better business strategy?

4. The concept of *customer-value-advantage* or rather of *customer-perceived-valued-advantage*: Business strategy developers are used to thinking and talking about differentiation and competitive advantage. However, the idea of competitive advantage is usually restricted to thinking narrowly about the insides of companies and what each has that is better than the other or what each does that is better than the other. But we believe that the idea of competitive advantage is about a company creating a customer-perceived-value advantage for itself

16

over its competitors, and in being able to sustain this because it does/has something that the competitor does not. So even if the costs of Company A are genuinely lower than that of Company B, it is a competitive advantage only if it is translated into a customer-perceived-value-advantage either in terms of lower prices for similar products or better quality for the same price.

5. Creating a 'business rivalry proposition' for the company that consumers accept as a 'why buy me' proposition.
6. Organizing the entire delivery mechanism of the business to be able to deliver the desired rivalry proposition (that is, fulfil its *why buy me* promise to customers).

NOTE

1. Net Promoter, NPS and Net Promoter Score are trademarks of Satmetrix Systems, Inc., Bain & Company and Fred Reichheld.

    The Net Promoter Score (NPS) is a management tool used to ascertain a firm's customer loyalty relationship. The company's NPS is calculated on the basis of a single question: How likely are you to recommend Company X to a friend or colleague? Customers respond on a 0–10 point rating scale, and based on their responses are categorized as Promoters, Passives or Detractors, indicating their level of enthusiasm towards the company. A company's NPS is calculated by subtracting the percentage of customers who are Detractors from the percentage of customers who are Promoters (see Figure 1.1). For more information, please visit www.netpromoter.com

Figure 1.1: Calculation of Net Promoter Score

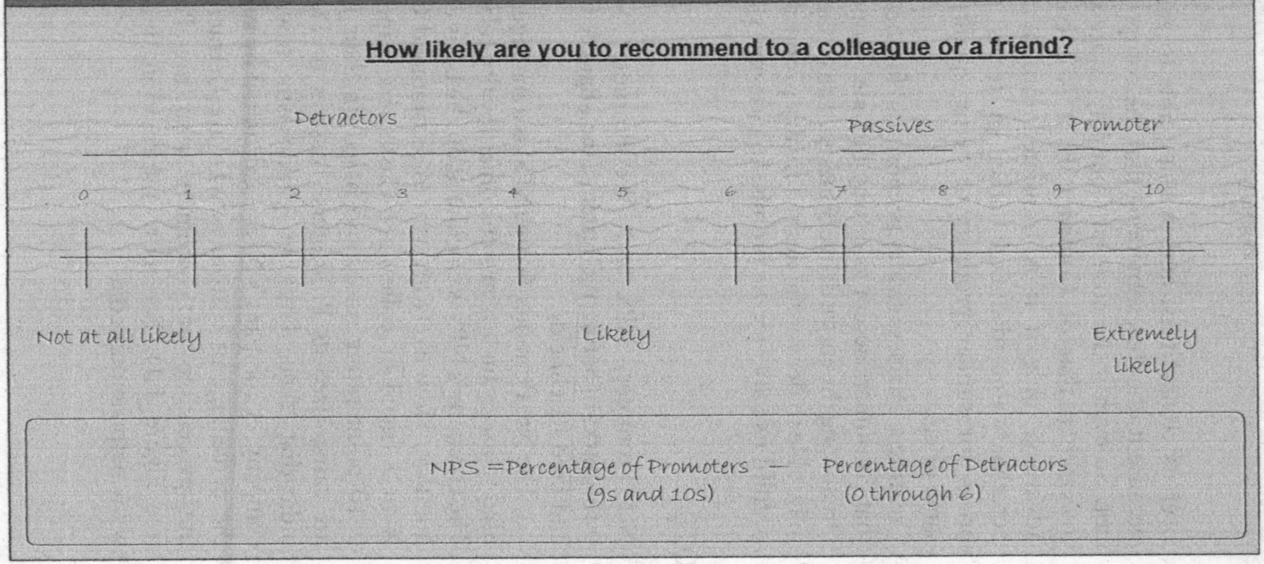

How likely are you to recommend to a colleague or a friend?

Detractors							Passives		Promoter	
0	1	2	3	4	5	6	7	8	9	10

Not at all likely   Likely   Extremely likely

NPS = Percentage of Promoters — Percentage of Detractors
(9s and 10s)   (0 through 6)

CHAPTER 2

Thinking about Business Strategy and Where the 'Customer' Fits into It

OH, NO! YET ANOTHER BUSINESS STRATEGY APPROACH AND FRAMEWORK?

The book *Harvard Business Essentials: Strategy* (2005: 30) says quite candidly: '[L]ook at the many text books on business strategy and you will find a cornucopia of strategy frameworks: low cost leadership, diversification, merger–acquisition, global customer focus, product leadership, vertical integration, flexibility, product/service differentiation, and so forth.' Henry Mintzberg, Bruce Ahlstrand and Joseph Lampel in their book, *Strategy Safari: A Guided Tour through the Wilds of Strategic Management* (1998), describe strategy formulation as the elephant and all of us as the blind people—alluding to the poem 'The Blind Men and the Elephant' by John Godfrey Saxe. The poem, as most readers will know, is about six blind men of Indostan who went to see an elephant, and each, depending on the part he touched, described the elephant as being just like a wall, a spear, a snake, a tree, a fan and a rope! The book then goes on to describe, in a similar vein, 'ten parts of our strategy formulation beast'. Each part relates to a 'school of thought' on what strategy is. Each school, therefore, has its own prescriptions about what should be the contents or elements of a strategy, what process should be used to develop it and what analysis of the external and internal environment it should be based upon.

We, therefore, recognize that most businesses already have a 'school of strategy' that they subscribe to and have a business strategy development approach that they use and have honed over time and aligned their organization systems and monitoring systems with. While we do present a total end-to-end approach of the school of strategy that we call Customer-Based Business Strategy (CBBS) that we hope companies will adopt, our objective is not to add one more framework to the menu already out there and suggest a total switch to that. Rather, our objective is to modestly, but zealously, get more and more companies to inject analyses and insights from the world of the customer into their existing business strategy development process. Our mental model is that there is a set of strands from which business strategy is already being woven, and we would like companies to include one stronger strand to the existing ones—the strand of being *customer-based*.

We hope that some of the bits and pieces of our CBBS framework will be extracted by readers and added as *plug and play* modules into their existing business strategy development process. We also hope that, if that is not possible, at least some of the customer analyses we suggest find their way into the bag of analyses that is normally done as part of the company's strategy development process.

In order to facilitate this, in this chapter, we will broadly review (or rather borrow from the literature of those who have already reviewed) different strategy development frameworks, understand the commonality among them, point to where being *customer-based* can fit in and enhance these frameworks and also point to the frameworks that we have been excited and guided by and that we used as building blocks to fashion our approach.

BUSINESS STRATEGY DEVELOPMENT: WHAT THE GURUS SAY

Almost all business strategy development approaches and frameworks are based on the skeleton or generic process shown in Figure 2.1.

Step 1: Set the business goals/objectives: A destination is defined and a time frame is set for where the business should get to and by when. There are many ways of doing this. Some companies define the goal for the next one year, others have a long-term vision or aspiration of what they want to become (incidentally, the phrase 'to become' is actually the hallmark of a vision statement) and have *rolled it back* year by year to the present. These destinations are always defined in financial terms, and often in non-financial terms as well (for example, 'become the dominant brand in XYZ space with 10 per cent points lead over the next' or 'be the most respected company for innovation', etc.). Thus, in most cases, specific and quantifiable goals are set and measurement metrics are laid out for *where to go*—if not for each year, then certainly for something like a three-year period. Often, tools like the Balanced Score Card are also used, which define the destination sought not just in terms of financial outcomes, but also in terms of factors such as customers, internal processes, learning and growth that influence these financial outcomes. (There is a recent

Figure 2.1: Generic Business Strategy Development Framework

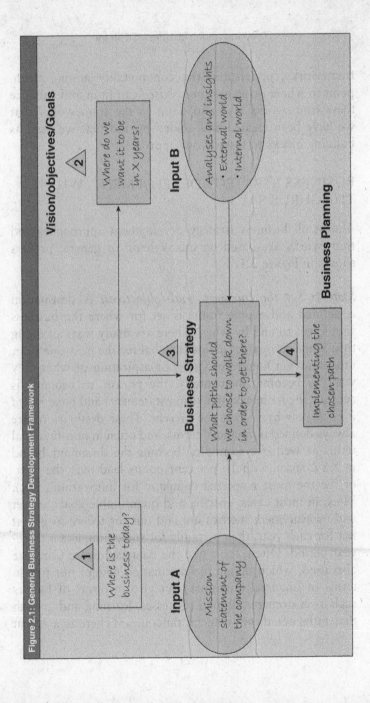

Vision/objectives/Goals

△2 Where do we want it to be in X years?

Input B

Analyses and insights
• External world
• Internal world

Business Strategy

△3 What paths should we choose to walk down in order to get there?

Business Planning

△4 Implementing the chosen path

△1 Where is the business today?

Input A

Mission statement of the company

body of strategy literature [see Appendix 1] that says that in a volatile world full of uncertainty, the 'destination' school of strategy does not make sense—because the destination itself may not exist in the future. Our view is that this does not refute classical strategy approaches but builds further on them.)

Step 2: Develop business strategy using a set of analyses to guide you: Business strategy is about identifying paths and choosing the ones that will get a business from where it is today to where it wants, or needs, to be. In order to do this, all strategy frameworks advocate understanding three important issues:

1. What is happening in the world outside (the external environment). This is about creating special types of terrain maps.
2. What is the situation inside the company (the internal environment). This is about sharply diagnosing what the problems and capabilities of the business are.
3. What is the mission of the company. The mission of a company is about the larger purpose it serves and the way it views itself and its work on a daily basis, for example, improving the nutritional status of children/ bringing good things to life/making the world a better place/catering to the everyday needs of people and delighting them, and so on. It circumscribes the paths that a business can choose to take and acts as a navigational aid for choices.

A recurrent theme in all strategy development approaches, and one which we will significantly build on in this book, is the need for an external orientation:

23

One of the trademarks of the modern planning approach is its external orientation.

—Hax and Majluf (1995)

The belief that strategic planning represented an automatic extension of what was done last year, and is dominated by financial objectives and spread sheets is inadequate. Rather, strategy development should look outside the business to sense changes and trends, threats and opportunities, and to create strategies that are responsive.

—Aaker (1998)

Operating a business without deeply understanding and actively managing both sides of the firm-customer relationship in an integrated fashion is somewhat akin to a physician treating patients without understanding their condition. . . . The way firms often manage businesses might even be called egotistical. . . . Egotistical firms may obsessively compare themselves with competitors, but the subject is the egotist, not the customer . . . . In Lewis Carroll's *Through the Looking Glass*, Alice is so fascinated by the images in the looking glass that she goes through it, into a world where backward logic and nonsense rule. Many business organizations . . . count themselves externally focused and do not recognize [that] in that looking glass, only the organization's products, resources, and processes can be clearly seen, not real life customers. . . . The strategy and marketing fields . . . provide a stream of varied rationalizations for a continuing focus on the organization's products and how to supply them, rather than on the resulting experiences the organization, in order profitably to grow, must deliver to customers.

—Lanning (2000)

Different companies express their business strategy differently. As Mintzberg et al. made clear in *Strategy Safari: A Guided Tour through the Wilds of Strategic Management* (1998), there is no single or unique way to say 'this is what a business strategy is or this is what a business strategy should contain' or 'this is how a strategy should be articulated'. One of the very popular schools of business strategy and one that many businesses love to use is what Mintzberg called the 'positioning school', also referred to as the 'industry structure-competitive positioning school' which says, very briefly and broadly, that where in the industry you are positioned (for example, where you figure in the growth–share matrix), automatically decides what kind of strategy you need to adopt, for example, 'low growth–high share' business should be harvested; a star business should be heavily invested in, a dog business should be divested, and so on.

Michael Porter, the towering proponent of the positioning school and author of *Competitive Advantage* (1985), describes generic strategies like *cost leadership*, *differentiation* and *focus* as routes to competitive advantage. There are others who build on this, as well as aggressively question this.

Professor Arnoldo C. Hax, a strategy guru whose strategy development framework is used by several Fortune 500 companies, says:

Concepts like strategic intent and core competencies represent a major challenge to the industry structure–competitive positioning paradigm. The major attack is directed at the importance of industry structure as the source of superior financial performance. Industry does not seem to matter any more. What truly distinguishes the performance of different firms competing in a given industry is not explained by the conditions of industry structure but rather by the capabilities and internal resources that the firms are deploying to differentiate from each other. (Hax and Majluf 1995)

Other scholars, like Michael J. Lanning, author of *Delivering Profitable Value* (2000), say that the success stories of the business strategies of some companies, for example, Southwest Airlines, 'contradict the standard strategic models' (for example, its strategy is a combination of several growth strategies like cost leadership, no frills and differentiation through focus). So it does appear that there are horses for courses, and that the strategy beast is different things to different people; hence strategy development could be as varied a belief system and art form as, say, weight loss diets or spirituality. But there are common goals and assumptions/logics behind all of them and it may make sense to start from there and explore what kind of *customer-based* thinking and doing can be injected at each level.

The *Harvard Business Essentials: Strategy* states that 'at bottom [of all these numerous strategy development frameworks], every for-profit entity aims for the same goal: to identify and pursue a strategy that will give it a defensible and profitable hold on some segment of the market.'

DIMENSIONS OF STRATEGY AND WHERE DOES 'CUSTOMER' FIT IN

Professor Arnoldo C. Hax, in his book *The Strategy Concept and Process* (co-authored with Nicholas S. Majluf

[1995]), identifies four critical dimensions of the concept of strategy:

1. *Strategy determines [establishes] the organizational purpose in terms of [defining] the long-term objectives, action programmes, and resource allocation priorities:* These objectives should have a certain sense of performance— nothing could be more destructive than an erratic reorientation of a firm's goals.

2. *Strategy selects [helps the company select] the businesses the organization is in or is to be in:* One of the central concerns of strategy is defining the business the firm is in or intends to be in (or should be in and is not, or is in but should not be in). The key for selection is segmentation. The essence of segmentation lies in selecting the customers that the business unit will be serving, and consequently, the competitors that they will be faced with.

3. *Strategy attempts to achieve a long-term sustainable advantage for the business over its key competitors* by responding appropriately to the opportunity and threats in the environment and to the strengths and weaknesses of the organization. This dimension of strategy is behind many of the 'positioning the firm in the industry' approaches to strategy. Michael Porter has been the dominant figure in shaping and communicating this framework for business strategy. (It is for achieving this long-term competitive advantage that several generic strategies are discussed and advised; for example, cost leadership, differentiation, focus, innovation, customer intimacy, etc.)

4. *Strategy is aimed at developing and nurturing the core competencies of the organization:* The basic notion about

core competencies is that they define the competitive strategy for the entire firm. What truly distinguishes the performance of different firms competing in an industry is not explained by conditions of industry structure, but rather by the capabilities and internal resources that the firms are deploying to differentiate themselves from each other.

Taking each of the four common concepts of strategy that Arnoldo C. Hax identified, let us examine the role of customer-based knowledge in each of these.

STRATEGY DETERMINES THE LONG-TERM OBJECTIVES AND RESOURCE ALLOCATION PRIORITIES

What added value can come from being customer-based? A question we frequently ask the boards of a companies, when faced with a plan from top management that says they want to be 'X' crore by 'Y' time is, 'How high is up? How do you know that this is not the right number and that your business has an entitlement that is actually much higher?' Often the current market size is not an indicator of the potential market. It is merely an indicator of the sum of the strategies and aspirations and resources of the existing players. And if the existing players happen to be myopic or imperfect or risk-averse, then the market remains underdeveloped.

This is especially true of emerging markets, and the only solution is to look beyond suppliers to end users and assess what opportunities they offer. In fact the problems that global companies face in emerging markets is under-investing, failing to grab as much opportunity as is possible and failing to beat consumers into submission.

Therefore, in order to set business objectives, a realistic grasp of the market environment in which the business operates or will operate in the future, is necessary. This requires a deep understanding of the fundamental determinants of market structure and customer behaviour relating to an entire need arena, not just the product–market currently served by the business (for example, transportation, not two-wheelers; all children, not just rich parents' children, etc.).

Here are some examples of customer-based setting of business objectives that could lead to a totally different answer from the supply-side view, and open up huge opportunities:

- For a country (market) where 21 million babies are born in a year, the current market size of the baby products FMCG and of branded apparel for children is very small in India (under USD 200 million). A new entrant setting long-term goals must understand why is it so. Is price point an issue? In the case of FMCG, is it the problem of global companies insisting on high margins, for example, Johnson & Johnson? Does the problem pertain to the lack of branding know-how amongst local apparel manufacturers and the dollar price conversion that global brands would like to get? What kind of special requirements do consumer feel babies have? Is there a huge opportunity for a certain kind of business proposition, and is that what your company can offer?
- Tortuous demand analyses are made on the car market in India, based on modelling the likely industry sales based on a set of macroeconomic, demographic, gasoline prices and road construction type variables. Companies then set targets of market share of the

forecasted industry sales and use them to define their long-term objective. If a company is a smaller player or a new player, the target market share is set much lower. But let us consider what would happen if we used a different consumer-based logic to define the long-term goals for a company. In many large cities in India, there is no organized taxi service despite many customers who have the money to spend on comfortable transport but do not own cars or if they do then drivers are scarce and the roads are tough to drive on. This points to a new and immediately available market to sell cars as taxis for a car company that is willing to make the effort to partner with others to build an ecosystem for offering a taxi service. This market could be as large and growing as that possible through fighting in a crowded market for personally owned or corporate owned cars.

- The ready-to-eat processed food market in India has been small and, though growing fast, disappointing in size, considering the large population and rapid income growths and changing patterns of family life and gender roles. However, before deciding what the long-term business objectives should be based on supply side industry size estimates, consider this:

    In India, we eat about one trillion chapatis a year but have no sale of ready-to-eat or ready-to-cook chapatis. Are consumers resistant? No, Indian women do not like the negative labour involved in making chapatis; but for some reason, no player in the processed food business has been able to offer 'husband acceptable quality' chapatis to the market at a reasonable price.

- Sometimes the market is well developed and looks very hard to crack because there is a formidable dominant market leader present, who seems to grow constantly. Hero Honda Splendour is one such player. When TVS, which is a successful but smaller competitor, wanted to set its revenue growth goals, the MD of the company relentlessly asked the question of why/whether Hero Honda was invincible, and how hard it would be to get the market share off it. The answer to the questions of what goals should be formulated and, hence, how much R&D effort should be put into the business stemmed from how one reads the success of Hero Honda Splendour. Was it really the solid Rock of Gibraltar that it appeared to be and hard to dent or was it an old brand, hollow from the inside, coasting along because no one had challenged it? And, in fact, were the customers actually ready to move on? When focus groups showed young people saying sanctimoniously: 'This is a sensible buy, one must not waste parents' money', or when they welcomed each new buyer of the product among their friends with, 'Oh! You too? Join the gang; just like us, you too have bought a Splendour!', it pointed to something *fishy*. Were consumers making a sub-optimal choice and rationalizing it for lack of a better option? Was the supposed bastion ready to crumble if stormed hard? It is answers to this, rather than market share trend graphs, that could help set realistic long-term objectives for the company.

- We worked with a client in the home fabrics business. He was mostly into exports, but wanted to grow in the domestic market as well. The question was: How large could the domestic business be, and, hence, what kind of resources and investments would be appropriate? The market leader was an old, established company, synonymous with bed linen, and had a large network of franchised outlets. The management logic was: 'If they, with their low prices and extensive distribution network cannot sell, then how can we?' If we look at this from a standard microeconomic industry analysis framework of 'industry structure–conduct–financial performance', this did not appear to be a business to set much hope on or pump more than modest resources into. However, when we analysed it in terms of a customer-based analysis of the business and look at consumer demand structure (who is buying as opposed to who is selling), consumer conduct and concerns (what are consumers doing rather than what the suppliers are doing, consumer behaviour drivers rather than suppliers' compulsions), and customer satisfaction (rather than profitability of industry), a very different picture emerged. We also noticed that every other part of the consumer's household had upgraded—modular kitchens, imported tiles, smart taps and other bathroom fittings, gadgets, etc. But the bed and bath furnishings had remained frozen in time. The customer base had received no communication or education about the product category in recent times and had been totally confused by the market leader's practice of selling the same product at a higher price through its showrooms, and at a lower price through low-end retailers who bought the same fabric and sewed bed sheets themselves (but branded these as a 'made from'), as well as hosting annual discount sales through all their showrooms selling the same goods available the year round at lower prices. Respondents in group discussions, when asked to enact the experience of going to franchised outlets, would enact a role play in which they started by waking up the retailer who would say: 'Come back later, this is siesta time!' When customers were shown samples of new age products for modern households, they were totally enthusiastic and very engaged. Clearly, the customer was neglected and was ready to be shaped. Clearly, the market leader's conduct had stunted market growth. The lesson: static or declining top lines of companies do not always reflect lack of customer demand or acceptance for the category. They reflect poor company conduct in fuelling demand. The long-term goals for a shaper organization would look very different from that of an adapter organization based on a supply-side view of the market. Thus, understanding opportunity and setting goals requires 'escaping the myopia of the served market and the current product concept and empathizing with human needs', as Hamel and Prahalad say in their book *Competing for the Future* (1996).

STRATEGY SELECTS THE BUSINESS THE ORGANIZATION IS IN OR IS TO BE IN

At a corporate-strategy level, this decision relates to which businesses the group should keep, which it should sell, how the available resources should be allocated across the different businesses, and so on. What value can being customer-based add on this count? This decision of whether or not, or what role an individual business should have in the overall business portfolio of a company, is usually made based on an assessment of attractiveness of the industry and the company's ability to compete in it. Based on supply-side variables, attractiveness is usually measured in terms of size of industry (i.e., sum total of sales of all suppliers), growth, profitability, etc.

However, the inclusion of consumer variables to measure attractiveness, such as intensity of felt need, willingness or ability to spend, consumers' perceived centrality of the product to their lives, etc., significantly de-risk or enhance the robustness of the attractiveness assessment. In fact, we should include variables such as customer loyalty and novelty seeking in the assessment of industry attractiveness. Competitiveness or ability to compete, which forms the other part of the assessment, is again often discussed in terms of supply-side variables like whether the competitor has a higher cost position, a more organized sales force, etc. What we recommend is that in addition to these, an assessment of competitiveness should include customer variables as well—what does the customer base his ultimate decision on? What is his decision model? How well is the competitor likely to deliver on each of the attributes or key decision factors used by the customers? And how well is the company itself likely to deliver on these? Is there a customer perception study data that can be used as an input into this judgement?

At an individual business unit level, this decision area becomes one of strategic market choice or the *where to compete* decision. It involves defining segments within a business and then prioritizing them in order to make resource allocation choices. This prioritization is based on an evaluation of the business attractiveness and the internal capabilities of the company to serve the business segment. Companies that define business segments in terms of simplistic supply-side variables like product types or technologies or competitor sales often end up being absent in emerging new businesses, unlike companies that define businesses in terms of customer variables. For example, business segments in the decorative paints business in India are typically defined as 'Household and Commercial', and within each, defined based on the type of product (emulsions, oil-based distempers, exteriors, enamels, etc.) and price level (premium, mid-tier, low tier). Redefining these business segments based on the purpose or benefit offered like 'speciality surface protection', 'fashion colours and textures', 'basic functionality and durability', and creating distinct Strategic Business Units (SBUs) for each could change the basis of competition altogether and give the company defining its businesses thus a significant first mover advantage in the minds of customers. However, identifying what these business segments could and should be, requires a deep and fundamental understanding of how consumers think about and buy paints, and is not easy to do because unlike normally used supply-side criteria like industry size, growth and profitability, such data is not available and has to be generated uniquely by the business.

STRATEGY ATTEMPTS TO ACHIEVE LONG-TERM SUSTAINABLE ADVANTAGE FOR THE BUSINESS OVER ITS KEY COMPETITORS

What value can being customer-based add on this count? The question that needs to be answered in the search for long-term sustainable competitive advantage is: What does this company have that the others it competes with do not have, which can be used to kill them in the marketplace? This again is a question that requires longer term visioning of how customers will evolve and what their choices of suppliers will eventually revolve around. It requires understanding how the customers process value. Is today's advantage going to be relevant tomorrow even if the company builds it into a long-term competitive advantage over the competitors? Eventually, the purpose of competitive advantage is to build

35

customer advantage, that is, advantage of use as perceived by customers.

Henry Mintzberg et al. have provided this example in their book *Strategy Safari: A Guided Tour through the Wilds of Strategic Management* (1998).

> Some of the most famous battles in business have been won not by doing things correctly, or following the accepted wisdom, but by breaking established patterns by creating new categories. Some firms stay at home and do competitive analysis; others go out there and create their own niches (leaving them with no competition to analyse!). BCG would have loved to call Honda a 'dog', when it entered the US motorcycle market in 1959. The market was well- established—big machines for black leather tough guys—and Honda was an insignificant player. It should have stayed away. But partly by creating a new motorcycle for small motorcycles driven by ordinary Americans, Honda became a star and took a huge share of a new growth business that it had created itself.

Mintzberg also quotes Richard Rumelt:

> In 1977, my MBA final exam on the Honda motorcycle case asked 'Should Honda enter the global automobile business?' It was a giveaway question—anyone who said 'yes' flunked. Markets were saturated, efficient competitors existed in Japan, Europe, the US. Honda had little or no experience in automobiles, and no auto distribution system. In 1985, my wife drove a Honda. (Mintzberg et al. 1998)

All the business strategy textbook exhortations about creating new markets, fighting against all odds, going where no competitor has, etc., can only come out of painstaking mapping of the entire potential customer universe, and a great deal of insight into what consumer needs are.

STRATEGY IS AIMED AT DEVELOPING AND NURTURING THE CORE COMPETENCIES OF THE ORGANIZATION

What value can being *customer-based* add on this count? How are core competencies linked with market and customers? The very definition of a core competency is as follows: *(a)* it should provide potential access to a wide variety of markets, *(b)* it should make a significant contribution to the perceived customer benefit and *(c)* it should be difficult for competitors to imitate.

Therefore, the purpose of nurturing core competencies—and even identifying or choosing them—is to enter and win in a range of new markets easily, to create customer benefits that competitors cannot match and, hence, create more value for the customer than competitors do.

SOME STRATEGY FRAMEWORKS THAT HAVE GUIDED US A GREAT DEAL

There are some business strategy frameworks that are far closer to the consumer or customer end of the business lens than the supplier end. We have drawn a lot of guidance and direction from them and used them as a basis for our framework. Hence, before laying out the CBBS framework, we would like to share these with the readers and discuss our extrapolations and interpretations of some of the concepts contained in them.

THE HAX 'UNIFIED CONCEPT OF STRATEGY' FRAMEWORK

This framework brings together two schools of strategy—the 'industry structure-competitive positioning' school and the 'strategic intent-core competency' school. It addresses two core questions:

1. *What is the business scope* (that is, *where* all in the market should the business compete)—which products to offer, which customers to serve, which geographies to serve.
2. *How to compete*—what core competencies to develop in order to achieve sustainable competitive advantage.

The Hax framework suggests a five-factor assessment of business segment attractiveness for the first decision—market factors, competitive factors economic and government factors, technological factors and social factors. In our CBBS framework, as we will discuss in subsequent chapters, we advocate taking one more step and understanding/assessing how each of these factors can impact the structure of consumer demand and consumer behaviour.

The McKinsey framework

Kevin P. Coyne and Somu Subramaniam of McKinsey & Company wrote in the *McKinsey Quarterly* (1996) suggesting 'a new definition of strategy'.

Strategy is a handful of decisions that:

- Drive or shape most of a company's subsequent actions.
- Are not easily changed once made.
- Have the greatest impact on whether the company's strategic objectives are met.

The handful of decisions are:

- Selecting the company's strategic posture.
- Identifying the source(s) of competitive advantage.
- Developing the business concept.
- Constructing tailored value delivery systems.

Selecting the Company's Strategic Posture

Strategic posture is an element of business strategy that, we believe, is very relevant to emerging markets. This builds on our earlier discussion about how business opportunities emerge when the consumer world is understood, but are not visible when supply-side analysis or 'industry' sizing is done. Depending on the extent of its ambition, a company can adopt one of three strategic postures: *adapting*, *shaping* and *reserving the right to play*.

Adapting is the most common choice made by companies. A company analyses its environment, then commits to a set of actions to conform to that environment. We often see this when strategy is decided based on the idea, 'doesn't everybody know, these are the rules of the market game of our industry'. Every new entrant—save the contrarian or the industry revolutionist or perhaps the customer based strategist—respects the existing rules, plays accordingly, struggles to differentiate at the margins, and almost never asks: 'Who made the rules anyway?'

Shaping consists of attempting to change the environment in a direction that will benefit the firm. Shapers invent entirely new products for which demand is only latent or develop entirely new ways to compete. In our experience, while almost every company wants to be a *shaper*, it is very difficult to be one if your reference point for action is your competitor set. In his book *Delivering Profitable Value* (2000: 119, 120), Michael J. Lanning, a former McKinsey partner, says of Southwest Airlines (SWA) strategy: 'How should one know whether to differentiate on all factors or only some? More importantly, differentiate in what ways?' He goes on to discuss the '*be a contrarian*' advice from Hamel and Prahalad (1994):

'[C]ontrarians find these conventions [hub-and-spoke model of airlines industry] and use them against orthodoxy-ridden incumbents. To discover the future, it is not necessary to be a seer, but it is absolutely vital to be unorthodox.' Lanning asks: 'But how would one recognize the hub-and-spoke convention as something to reject? The hub-and-spoke *was* superior to a point-to-point convention at that time.' He goes on to add, tongue-in-cheek: 'Luckily, King [the Southwest Airlines CEO] didn't mistake wings [in the aircraft] a convention of the orthodoxy ridden incumbents to reject.' Lanning's assessment of SWA's success is as follows:

> SWA is focused on an intended passenger, who makes a particular kind of trip, which the industry has abandoned [those making a short trip]. Prior to SWA's arrival in a market, typically more than half of such trips were made by car or by bus. SWA's value delivery system is entirely shaped to deliver superior

value profitably to this short-trip customer. (Lanning 2000: 119, 120)

SWA's business strategy was clearly that of a *shaper* and was *customer-based*, and not competitor-centred. It started its strategy development with a segment of customers (potential) who were not flying and it offered them a value proposition that was superior to their current mode of travel, and it created a value delivery system, or rather innovated one, which would deliver the proposition to customers and create profit for the company. That this was a new model for the industry, is only incidental. Closer home, Nirma was a shaper, Titan was a shaper, Nano is definitely a shaper. What they all have in common is that: *(a)* they are market creators unfettered by analyses of what the current market size is and what it is forecasted to grow to; *(b)* they recognize that current product markets are the size they are not because Indians are too unevolved to have desires, but because they do not have enough money; and *(c)* they start with a potential customer base (and not a current industry size), they define a price and a quality that customers will accept, and then challenge themselves to deliver it profitably. It is here that many companies, especially MNCs, fail badly. They set a challenge price above which they must not go, but they refuse to accept the value processing algorithm that customers have inside their heads, and what features the new-age customer will or will not sacrifice, for a lower price tag.

Reserving the right to play is a non-committal posture. It consists of doing the minimum required to keep open the possibility of becoming a strong player later. It is not the same as taking no action at all; rather it is an investment, it is learning. We find many MNCs that are not sure whether this market is ready for them or not, but want to hedge their bets. The simplest example is the number of foreign retailers operating here through franchise arrangements with local businesses.

Strategic posture, according to us, is not just about what risk appetite a company has, but about what consumer insight a company has that helps it to place the risky bet that a market is ready for being shaped, that is, that consumers are ready to have their behaviour and their thinking shaped.

We have discussed some of these examples in earlier chapters. We often tell our clients: 'First, let us agree on what we need to believe about consumers in order to believe that this market is ready for shaping. Then, let us go out and test to what extent those conditions prevail in the consumer world.' In order to conclude whether the packaged food market in India is ready to be shaped, we need to understand what women are doing and thinking and feeling, and how this is changing with respect to feeding their families, shopping for goods, etc. We need to study the eating patterns and satisfaction levels at a micro level (the college student from Bihar studying at a regional engineering college in Warangal or the Punjabi boy working in an IT company in Pune); we need to ask why no competitor has ever managed to crack this market; we need to understand family demographics and lifestyles carefully and other macro forces at work; and we need to see into the future to determine how this will change based on what leading-edge consumers are doing.

DEVELOPING THE BUSINESS CONCEPT

The *business concept* is an idea that excites us a lot. It is about defining what game the business will play in the market. 20–20 cricket? Kabaddi? Lawn tennis? This framework defines it as 'an integrated and consistent set of

42

decisions relating to where, how, and when to compete in the market'. *Where* refers to market segment priorities that we have discussed earlier. *How* is the way by which the business will create consumer *value advantage* compared to competitors—again a concept that we have discussed earlier. *When* is the question of the right timing to compete in the market.

CONSTRUCTING TAILORED VALUE DELIVERY SYSTEMS

The *tailored value delivery system* is a concept that inspires us a great deal—the idea that a business is a value delivery system and must be designed in order to deliver on the promises made to customers. So, for example, if Johnson & Johnson's promise to customers is that their business will always provide 'pure', 'mild' and 'gentle' products to customers, then even the front-line junior salesman of the company must be empowered to remove dusty or shop-soiled expensive packs from the top shelf and replace them instantly. If Titan watches came into the Indian market offering 'international quality and style', then it had to upgrade the retailing ambience in the country—one cannot deliver international quality and style or even communicate it through grotty little watch shops in Flora Fountain! And the French and Italian designers should be employed right up front, no matter what they cost!

Michael J. Lanning suggests that the idea of the value delivery system is at the core of enabling an organization to deliver profitable value—superior value to its customers that can be profitable for the business. He conceptualizes a business as a value delivery system, rather than the conventional idea that a business is a collection of activities such as sales, marketing, manufacturing, etc. The concept of a business as a value delivery system is illustrated in Figure 2.2. In this concept, there are three parts to a business. The first part is the value proposition that it offers its consumers or customers as a reason for buying; the second part is the way it organizes itself internally in order to be able to deliver the proposition, that is, the delivery system; and finally, the way it communicates the proposition to its many stakeholders including its current and potential customers.

Therefore, strategy development revolves around generating and choosing value propositions (which deliver customer perceived value better than competitors, and profitably too); designing all functions, products or services, and relationships single-mindedly around the chosen value proposition; the delivery of this proposition determines all revenues and all costs.

DAVID AAKER'S FRAMEWORK

According to Aaker (1998), a business strategy, sometimes termed 'competitive strategy' or simply 'strategy', is defined by six elements or dimensions. The first four apply to any business unit even if it exists by itself. The remaining two are introduced when the business unit exists in an organization with other business units.

A business strategy includes a determination of:

1. *The product market in which the business is to compete*: The scope of a business is determined by the products it offers and chooses not to offer, by the markets it serves and those that it does not serve, competitors it chooses to compete or not compete with, and by its level of vertical integration. (All these decisions, taken in an

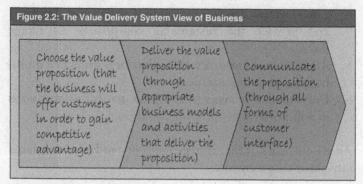

Figure 2.2: The Value Delivery System View of Business

Choose the value proposition (that the business will offer customers in order to gain competitive advantage)

Deliver the value proposition (through appropriate business models and activities that deliver the proposition)

Communicate the proposition (through all forms of customer interface)

Source: Adapted from Lanning (2000).

integrated fashion, result in the *where to compete* part of the 'business concept' that the McKinsey framework talked about.)

2. *The level of investment*: It is useful to conceptualize the alternatives (although there are obvious variations) as:

   (i)   Invest to grow
   (ii) Invest only to maintain the existing position
   (iii) Milk the business by minimizing investment
   (iv) Recover the assets by liquidating or divesting

   (In the Hax framework, the levels of investment are further divided into maintain aggressively, maintain selectively, build aggressively, build selectively, prove viability and competitive harasser. We will discuss these in the next chapter.)

3. *The functional area strategies* needed to compete in the select product markets.

4. *The strategic assets or skills* that underlie the strategy and provide the sustainable competitive advantage (SCA).
5. *Allocation of resources across business units* in a multi-business unit organization.
6. *Development of synergistic effects across business units* in a multi-business unit organization.

All six elements of the strategy concept can be encapsulated into three core elements:

1. The product-market investment decision that encompasses the product–market scope of business strategy, its investment intensity and the resource allocation over multiple businesses. (Comment: This is what some refer to as the *where to compete* decision.)
2. The functional area strategies—what you do. (Comment: A part of this is what some strategy frameworks refer to as *how to compete*.)
3. The basis of sustainable competitive advantage to compete in these markets. (Comment: A part of this is what was discussed in the context of a tailored value delivery system.)

GEORGE DAY'S FRAMEWORK

'Strategy is a very elastic term, with so many meanings in common that it has almost lost meaning', says Professor George Day, an authoritative and widely respected voice in the area of marketing and strategic management, creator of the phrase 'market driven', and author of the classic *Market Driven Strategy: Processes for Creating Value* (originally published in 1990, and now in its 21st reprinting). He defines the concept of strategy as 'integrated action in pursuit of competitive advantage'. We find his definition simple and compelling.

According to Professor Day, the core of strategy should include the following:

- **A business definition** that describes the market arena that the business has chosen to compete in (especially the customer needs to be satisfied, the technology used to satisfy these needs, and the customer segments to target). [This corresponds to the *where to compete*, or the strategic market priorities description we have seen in other frameworks.]
- **The strategic thrusts** that specify how the business intends to gain and sustain a competitive advantage and the pattern of investments that will be required to support strategy. [This corresponds to the *how to compete*, prioritization of business segments, levels of investments, and strategic posture that other frameworks have talked about.]
- **The objectives**, which are commitments to performance results that the business team expects to achieve in the future.

Professor Day's 4As' framework says that 'strategies are directional statements where the direction is set by four choices'. These are:

- Arena: The markets to serve and the customers to target.
- Advantage: The positioning theme that differentiates the business from that of the competitors.

47

- Access: The communication and distribution channels used to reach markets.
- Activities: The appropriate scale and scope of activities to be performed.

This is a first-cut version of Michael J. Lanning's concept of a value delivery system—where 'appropriate' is determined by what value proposition is promised to the customer.

'These choices are highly interdependent—change one and all the other elements of the strategy have to be changed.'

KENICHI OHMAE'S FRAMEWORK

Our favourite strategist is Kenichi Ohmae, author of *The Mind of the Strategist: The Art of Japanese Business*, former McKinsey director and guru at large. In a brilliant article in the *Harvard Business Review* titled 'Getting Back to Strategy' (1988), which we have discussed in the previous chapter, he makes the point that 'the heart of strategy is not about beating the competitor but [about] adding value to the customer and avoiding the competitive battle altogether'. This is the heart of our philosophy and that of this book on CBBS. The mission of business strategy is to 'create wealth for the company by creating value for the customer—in a sustainable environment and competition proof way'.

In his book, *The Mind of the Strategist: The Art of Japanese Business* (1991), Ohmae says:

> In the construction of any business strategy, three players must be taken into account: the corporation itself, the customer, and the competition.

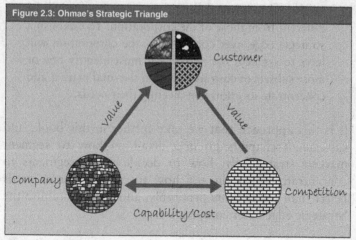

Figure 2.3: Ohmae's Strategic Triangle

Source: Adapted from Ohmae (1991).
Note: Value = $\sum$Benefits − $\sum$Cost (as perceived by the consumer).

Each of these *Strategic 3Cs* is a living entity with its own interests and objectives. We shall call them collectively, the strategic triangle [see Figure 2.3].

Seen in the context of the strategic triangle, the job of the strategist is to deliver superior value to customers, as compared to competition, and at a profit to the company. A successful strategy is one that ensures a better or stronger matching of corporate strengths to customer needs, than is provided by competitors.

In a free economy, no given market remains homogeneous, since each customer group will tend to want a slightly different service or product. But the corporation cannot reach out to all customers with equal effectiveness; it must distinguish easy to access customers from hard-to-reach ones. Moreover, the competitor's abilities to respond to customer needs and to cover different customer groups will be different from those of the corporation. To establish a strategic edge over competition, the corporation will have to segment the market—it must identify one or more subsets of customers within the total market and concentrate its efforts on meeting their needs.

It is this approach that we take further in this book, and subsequent chapters go into detail on how to segment markets strategically, how to decide which segments to concentrate efforts on and how to meet customer needs better than competitors profitably, and hence, establish the 'strategic edge' over competitors.

SUMMARY

In this chapter, we have discussed the popular frameworks and approaches for developing business strategy and the commonalities between them. We then presented some business strategy frameworks that are more customer oriented and pointed out where *market* and *customer* fit into each. The dominant themes that emerge from all frameworks are that business strategy is about:

1. Setting goals and objectives.
2. Deciding *where/which* business/*which* market/*which* customer segment to compete in with *what* intensity and resources.
3. Deciding how to create consumer and, hence, competitive advantage.
4. Delivering on all these through an appropriate business design, tailor-made for the choices made for *where* and *how to compete*.

We now move on to presenting the CBBS framework, born out of these, and explaining the principles and processes of each element of the framework.

Appendix

Strategy as Simple Rules

By Kashleen M. Eisenhardt and Donald N. Sull
Harvard Business Review, 1 January 2001, hbr.org/product/ strategy- as-simple-rules

The authors contend that 'the new economy's most profound strategic implication is that companies must capture unanticipated fleeting opportunities in order to succeed'.

Therefore, they say that while the strategic logic of the 'positioning school' (i.e., where in the industry do you want to position yourself?) is to 'build a fortress and defend it' and ask the strategic questions 'where should we be', the strategic logic of the 'strategy-as-simple-rules' school is to pursue opportunities and ask the strategic question 'how should we proceed'.

In our view, the questions 'where the business wants to be in X years' and 'what are its business goals and objectives' are equally relevant in times of uncertainty. If they are defined as the financial and market health goals of a business (e.g., become the market leader and the most preferred brand in the customer segment of rural customers' health care expenditure), then no matter which school of strategy one adopts, the goal remains valid. If, however, the goal of 'where does the business want to be X years from now' is defined in terms of product segments, as in 'be the leader in desktop applications and group voice communication', then in the uncertain world of technology, desktop and group voice communications could both become irrelevant!

The strategy-as-simple-rules school advocates a set of navigators and choice principles based on which opportunities can be continuously spotted and pursued. The 'where and how to compete in the market' dimensions that we will discuss in the next chapter onwards merely become continuous activities, not activities decided once in three years. The framework and concepts remain valid. In fact, we believe that a customer-based view of the world will enable easier spotting and pursuit of new opportunities than a product-based view of the world.

STRATEGY UNDER UNCERTAINTY

This article by Hugh G. Courtney, Jane Kirkland and S. Patrick Vigurie in *The McKinsey Quarterly* spells out yet another approach to developing strategy in uncertain conditions. 'The traditional approach to strategy requires precise predictions and thus often leads executives to underestimate uncertainty. This can be downright dangerous.'

In this approach, the authors suggest the different kinds of uncertainty that exist should be analysed and categorized as 'a clear enough future', 'alternative futures' (where which one will prevail is hard to predict but the options are clear), 'a range of futures' and 'time uncertainty'.

The authors suggest that different 'strategic postures' and a 'portfolio of bets' can be placed to deal with these different levels of uncertainty rather than placing a single bet on where and how to compete based on a singular view of what the future market and industry will look like.

This portfolio of bets is classified by them as big bets, options and no regrets moves.

Therefore, this approach suggests developing business strategy for each of these different types of uncertainty scenarios and then tracing each one as a bet, deciding what the size and nature of the bet should be.

CHAPTER 3

The Customer-Based Business Strategy (CBBS) Framework

Our approach to business strategy is based on the view that a business is a value delivery system, a concept that we discussed in Chapter 2 in the context of the McKinsey and Michael Lanning frameworks.

In our approach, business strategy has a front end called the business-market strategy and a back end which consists of all the functional area strategies developed, such that they are aligned to the market strategy.

Our mental model of business strategy is a train (see Figure 3.1). The engine pulling the whole train along is the *business-market strategy*, and it is this engine that determines which paths in the market the business is going to travel along (or walk down, as we phrased it earlier). The rest of the functional area strategies (finance, manufacturing, HR, etc.) are like compartments of the train, that must stay on the paths that the engine is defining and not forge their own tracks. We believe that the process of developing business strategy should first of all 'set' the business-market strategy. Then, the rest of the business

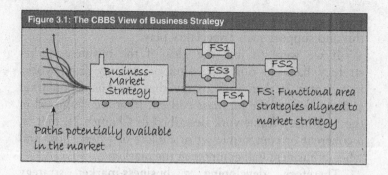

Figure 3.1: The CBBS View of Business Strategy

strategy elements—how do we finance, do we make or buy, who should we acquire, what manufacturing strategy should we have, what businesses should we sell, how should we unlock the potential of our assets, etc. flows from the business-market strategy: the thought here being that all the 'inside-out' actions of a business should support its 'outside' intentions in the market. We teach an M&A case in our course, about a regional brewing company wanting to go global and grow. It needs to choose from a lot of options available—merge, acquire, have a marketing joint venture for certain geographies, etc. Our class inevitably dives into financial analysis to determine which option is the best to pursue. From a business strategy point of view, however, in the absence of a clear business-market strategy, the choices made on this basis are not really strategic. If the company decides to play in the market by exploiting its unique knowledge of brewing, and wants to win by creating unique local brews, then merging with a big global brand, no matter how attractive the deal is, is the wrong thing to do. It should acquire local brewers in each country. If it decides to play by showcasing its country of origin like Mexican beer or French wine do, then it makes sense to acquire or merge with a company that can offer them global distribution for this and support such a speciality play.

If we were to link the idea of the business-market strategy back to our discussion of strategy frameworks in Chapter 2, then we can say that the business-market strategy defines the *business concept* (that we discussed in the McKinsey framework described in Chapter 2), that is, a coherent or compatible set of choices of where, how and when a business will compete in the market.

Therefore, developing a business-market strategy involves:

- Deciding which parts of the market the business will play in and with what priority (where to compete).
- Deciding what value proposition to offer consumers—this will be different for each chosen part of the market, because consumers will have different needs and the competitors will be different too (how to compete).
- Designing the tailored value delivery system for ensuring that the business delivers its promise to customers. We discussed this in Chapter 2 as a part of Michael J. Lanning's framework of Delivering Profitable Value. If the business is offering multiple value propositions because it is serving many different parts of the market, then it will have multiple value delivery systems.

The functional strategies are all about organizing the insides of the organization to be able to deliver the chosen value proposition perfectly and efficiently to the chosen customer segment (see Box 2 in Figure 2.2). The functional strategies are also about communicating the value proposition of the business to the relevant customers at each and every point of interface with customers (see Box 3 in Figure 2.2).

To sum up, the business-market strategy is at the very heart of business strategy and is about what the business will do or how and where it will play in the world *outside*. The functional strategies and the tailored value delivery systems are about what this business will do or how it will play in the world *inside*. This book focuses on how to develop business-market strategy in the belief that once this is 'set', then all other 'concerted activities' that an organization needs to perform as part of its business strategy, will automatically become clear and more logically obvious to decide.

A BUSINESS-MARKET STRATEGY IS NOT THE SAME AS A FUNCTIONAL MARKETING STRATEGY

There is considerable confusion in the minds of people between a business-market strategy and a functional marketing strategy (which is what the term 'marketing strategy' is more commonly used for). The differences between these two were discussed in Chapter 1. Let us recapitulate these in Table 3.1 once before moving on.

Ironically, this confusion particularly occurs in FMCG companies, which, because they have a strong functional

Table 3.1: Business-Market and Functional Marketing Strategies	
Business-Market Strategy	**Functional Marketing Strategy**
Developed for the business unit as a whole—the unit at which business strategy is developed, which has an independent P&L.	Developed for a category or brand—the unit of marketplace action.
Concerned with long-term competitive advantage for the firm.	Concerned with design of marketing programme or marketing mix.
Shapes business direction by taking cues from the market.	Implements business direction in the market.

marketing ethos, tend to think of their business as being a collection of brands and their business strategy as a collection of brand strategies. However, they do not go all the way and think of their brands as business units which require a business strategy. Here is an example that illustrates this confusion: We once worked with a well-known FMCG company in the business of household cleaning. Their product range comprised a brand of antiseptic, that we will, for this discussion, call Dash—Dash antiseptic liquid, Dash antiseptic soap, both on the 'kills germs' position; and a brand of toilet cleaner that we will call Hiss. They wanted to develop a business strategy to drive quantum growth, but in their minds, the business strategy was mixed up with the brands' functional marketing strategies, which were about making the *germ kill* proposition more appreciated by large parts of India, where they felt people were not educated or evolved enough. Their efforts were therefore focused on understanding how best to make consumers appreciate the benefits, of 'germ kill' products and be willing to pay for them—they looked at product optimization, SKU range, pricing, etc. and spent a lot of time developing and testing communication of germ kill benefits and the competitive superiority of their brand and this dimension. An external analysis of the consumer world, however, threw up an interesting business direction that was far removed from 'germ kill'.

A booming economy that had been continuously posting growth rates of the kind that India had never ever experienced before resulted in significant growth in household income, even at the lowest income strata. Thus, there was suddenly a large mass of people in rural India who had just escaped poverty. What this meant was that there was a new and interesting consumer segment that had come into existence that was likely to be extremely receptive to cleaning products because the way those above in the social ladder differentiated themselves from those below was through the level of cleanliness in their homes. In fact, even in slums and chawls, the slightly better-off signal their superiority through cleaner, better-maintained houses, even though all of them live in the same dreary one-room tenements.

Added to this income growth and the desire to signal their newfound social mobility was the fact that many of them started sending their children to school—the first generation in the family to actually go to school. They were formally taught about hygiene and health in school, and came home with 'teacher said' diktats about cleanliness of the home and personal hygiene.

A third driver of hygiene consciousness was that the average number of years of education of mothers and housewives had increased substantially compared to the generation before it.

If that was the story of the mass market of most rural households and low-income urban households, the story at the upper-income end of urban households was equally interesting. Women were rapidly reorganizing their housework and their priorities, driven by the fact that most mothers were now well educated, and very ambitious for their children, who were facing unbelievably competitive environments and needed a lot more parental attention. Fathers were commuting longer distances, working harder and were generally less available, thus increasing the load on the mothers. The women were also either working outside the home or doing more (as they described it), outdoor work, etc. Clearly, time had to be managed better and they were doing a portfolio rationalization of their various chores or roles. They were choosing on the basis of how much effort was required for each, and what appreciation it got them from the family and the outside world. By this logic, cooking was still high priority. Though high on effort, it was also high on appreciation. So was supervising children's homework and extracurricular activities.

Household cleaning was however high on effort and low on appreciation, and hence, was outsourced to the maid. However, supervising the maid so that the house did not run to seed and still looked good was a big area of concern. So the equilibrium they got to was to lay down a set of protocols or processes for cleaning for the maid to follow. They did not actively supervise the outcome, but just asked the maid once in a while whether she was following the processes. ('Did you move the furniture and sweep behind the sofas?!') This is not hard to believe—cleaning is a ritual in India, where even cow dung is purified by sprinkling water around it and a dip in a very polluted but holy river is supposed to cleanse a lifetime of sins!

Clearly, reading all these factors together, it was obvious that the market was ripe for the company to make a big and broad-based thrust into the house/home cleaning and hygiene space through designing new products and constructing customized portfolios of products and services, targeting consumers at different points of the income spectrum. The company could have achieved the quantum growth it desired by occupying the strategic position of a knight in shining armour and taking charge of the important household activity that housewives and mothers did not want to do any more, and could not wait to jettison, which they were delegating to their maids with no assurance of the desired outcome.

However, the company saw its business through the narrow lens of the Dash brand and the Hiss brand; and through the narrow lens of *germ kill* that these brands were known for—a classic inside-out view of the world; strategy run by functional marketing folks, not business leaders. They thought of their strategy as growing Dash and Hiss, extending the brand, etc., and in terms of estimating what they needed to do to make *germ kill* more relevant. For those of us who live in India, in environments awash with germs, the futility of this is quite apparent. The company missed the wood for the trees, and lost two big emerging opportunities for the business as a whole; one that could have been built targeting the upper income households around the value proposition of: 'Outsource your home cleaning to us while you do other important things. We will ensure quality no matter how lax your maid is and how busy you are to supervise her.' And the other targeted at the lower income end of the consumer spectrum around the value proposition of 'Make a social statement about your family's ascent with a few *must have* products and rituals that are the signal of people on the ascent'.

B2B companies and consumer durables companies, where the product or service and not its marketing is the hero of the business, are ironically more easily able to see the difference between a business-market strategy and a functional marketing strategy than FMCG companies.

To recap, a business-market strategy is about defining what game the business, as a whole, will play in which part of the playground, that is, the market, and how and why it will win. Therefore, a business-market strategy is about reading markets and defining a business direction, as distinct from a functional marketing strategy, which is about executing or implementing the chosen business direction in the market.

Figure 3.2: The Three Levels of Marketing

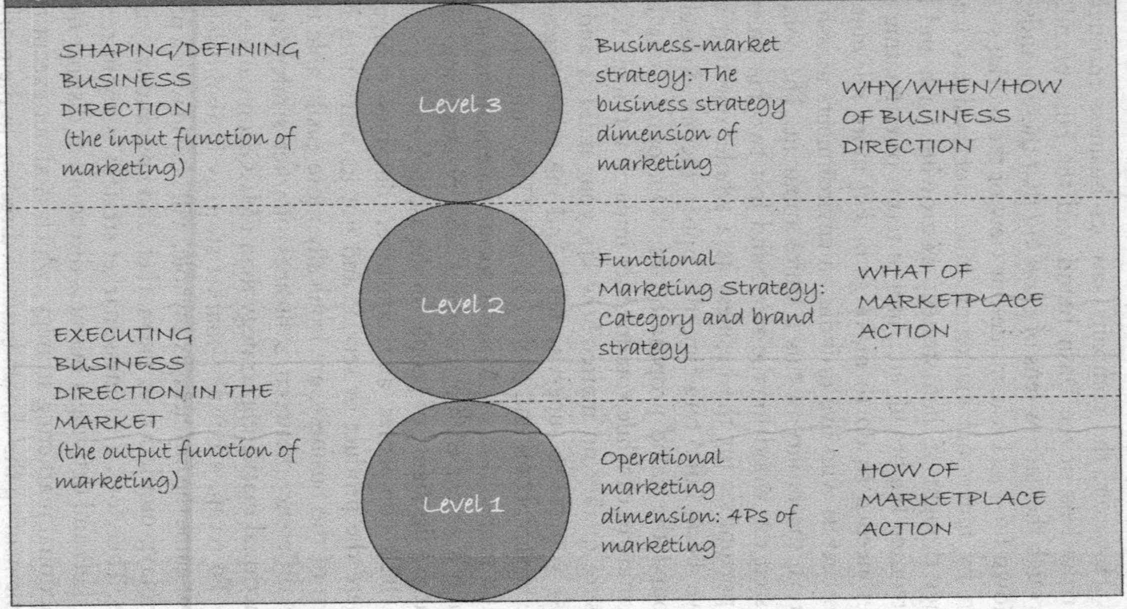

SHAPING/DEFINING
BUSINESS
DIRECTION
(the input function of
marketing)

Level 3

Business-market
strategy: The
business strategy
dimension of
marketing

WHY/WHEN/HOW
OF BUSINESS
DIRECTION

Level 2

Functional
Marketing Strategy:
Category and brand
strategy

WHAT OF
MARKETPLACE
ACTION

EXECUTING
BUSINESS
DIRECTION IN THE
MARKET
(the output function of
marketing)

Level 1

Operational
marketing
dimension: 4Ps of
marketing

HOW OF
MARKETPLACE
ACTION

Source: Adapted from Ramchander (2002).

To use our games and playgrounds analogy, the business-market strategy defines the playground, the game and the ways of playing it in order to win; the functional marketing strategy maps out all the things needed to actually play the game out there. To use a cricket analogy, the business-market strategy decides that it will be a 20–20 game to be played, that it will be won with an offensive game, played by spin bowlers putting pressure on the batsmen. The job of translating this into action and figuring out the order of bowlers, deciding what kind of pressure to put on each batsman, how frequently to change bowlers, setting up the field correctly, etc. is what functional marketing does.

One of our colleagues on this journey, the late S. Ramchander describes this difference clearly and succinctly in his book *Ascending the Value Spiral* (2002). The version we have adapted is described in Figure 3.2.

Ramchander talks of the three levels of marketing that are interconnected with each other. Level 3 marketing is about the input function of marketing—about reading markets to *shape* or *define* business direction, that is, the business-market strategy. Levels 1 and 2 are about the *output* function of marketing or the functional marketing strategy, that is, implementing the chosen business direction in the market. Level 2 marketing is usually about category and brand strategy, which is the marketing director's domain and relates to developing the strategy for marketplace action, the 'what' of marketplace action. Re-launch or not re-launch? A new brand variant or not? What should the brand architecture be? What sort of speed of product upgrades should we be doing? Should we pincer our competitor with brands priced above and below him? Should we start or respond to price cuts or advertising increases by our competitors? How do we run multiple distribution channels that do not conflict with each other? And so on. Level 1 marketing is about designing the 'how of marketplace action', for example, designing promotions, advertising, trade management, etc. In the case of B2B companies, especially those with few and large customers, we find that Levels 1 and 2 are merged and designed for individual customers. However, as a result of the comfort of having so much customer intimacy at the individual level, Level 3 marketing, which requires stepping back and aggregating knowledge and perspectives across individual customers to determine the companies' business-market strategy or winning 'game' in the market is rarely done by B2C companies. We are in no way suggesting that the output function of marketing, that is, implementing the business strategy in the marketplace, is not a critical function or not 'real' marketing. We are merely saying that there is another very important dimension to the discipline of marketing that needs to be done for aiding business strategy and is not done in a systematic fashion—in fact is not even considered relevant to business strategy.

We hope we have been able to clearly distinguish business-market strategy from functional marketing strategy, and have elevated its relevance to the boardroom and the CEO's office, and distinguished it from the types of functional marketing strategy decisions that get taken in the marketing manager's cabin or even in the CMO's office!

DEVELOPING THE BUSINESS-MARKET STRATEGY

In the CBBS framework, the articulation of the business strategy is centred around two connected buckets (Figure 3.3):

Figure 3.3: The Customer-Based Business Strategy Framework

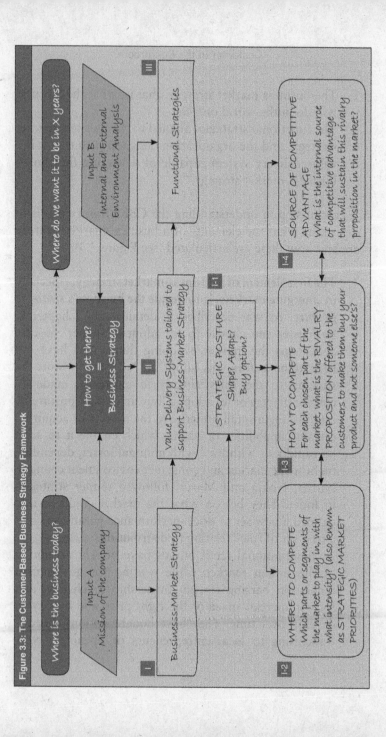

Where is the business today?

Where do we want it to be in x years?

How to get there? = Business Strategy

Input A
Mission of the company

Input B
Internal and External Environment Analysis

I Business-Market Strategy

II Value Delivery Systems tailored to support Business-Market Strategy

III Functional Strategies

I-1 STRATEGIC POSTURE
Shape? Adapt?
Buy option?

I-2 WHERE TO COMPETE
Which parts or segments of the market to play in, with what intensity? (also known as STRATEGIC MARKET PRIORITIES)

I-3 HOW TO COMPETE
For each chosen part of the market, what is the RIVALRY PROPOSITION offered to the customers to make them buy your product and not someone else's?

I-4 SOURCE OF COMPETITIVE ADVANTAGE
What is the internal source of competitive advantage that will sustain this rivalry proposition in the market?

1. The business-market strategy, that is, what the business will do in the world *outside*.
2. The functional strategies aligned to the business-market strategy, and the organization designed such that it is a value delivery system capable of delivering the chosen business-market strategy.

A crucial step in understanding the CBBS framework is to determine what the elements of a business-market strategy are and how these are articulated (see Figure 3.3):

1. **The first element of a business-market strategy, especially in emerging markets, is to decide the business's *strategic posture*.** As was described in detail in the Chapter 2, businesses can choose to (a) adopt a 'shaper' posture and shape the market by doing things that have not been done before, (b) adopt an 'adapter' posture by sticking to the rules already in existence, made by current players or (c) adopt a 'buy an option' posture by establishing a small presence in the market or acquiring certain capabilities or assets, which enable it to scale up rapidly or withdraw with minimal losses, depending on how the market and consumer environment changes. Nirma, Nokia and Maruti followed *shaper* strategies in India. They bet on what the market could be and defined a new set of price–performance parameters and a new set of rules relating to distribution.

   International retail brands have bought an option in the Indian market while waiting for government regulation barring foreign ownership to change, and for commercial space of the right price and quality to develop over time. They have bought options through franchising to local entrepreneurs or opening a very limited number of stores with strong media presence and other such methods. Some companies are clear that shaping a market is not what they will do. However, there are several others, especially global companies from the developed world entering emerging markets, who would like to shape markets and gain significantly from this. Unfortunately, they often lose a lot of money and gain little market success doing this because they do not read the market first to understand what customers are thinking and doing, and how latent their satisfaction or dissatisfaction or pain points are in terms of their current methods of fulfilling needs.

As we tell some of our clients, *shaping a market is not about either trying to beat it into submission with marketing aggression or educating it to behave in a particular way*. The market has to be ready for being shaped, that is, customers have to be *ready to see superior value in something and should discover good reasons why they want to shed their old ways* of doing things and switch to new ways of doing the same thing.

2. **The second part of a business-market strategy is the decision of *where to compete* or *where to play* in the market.** Markets are made up of many different segments and the *where*—to-play decision relates to deciding which parts or segments of the market the business wants to play in and with what intensity. This decision is often referred to as 'deciding strategic market priorities'. Visually, what a strategic market prioritization would entail is shown in Figure 3.4.

The different shapes refer to different parts of the market—for example, large, medium, and small corporate in the case of banks; or long haul versus short haul in the case of a freight company; or PC versus mobile applications; and so on. We used to pose the market choice question to our clients as: If all these segments of the market/businesses were your children and they were drowning, and in order to save some children you had to let go of some, which of them would you save and which would you regretfully let go? Over the years, we found that our clients were having difficulty in answering this because resources have become more easily available through credit and capital markets. We now ask the question as: If you did not have enough money to educate all your children well, which child would you send to Harvard, which to a good local college and which would you probably not send to college at all?

There are several portfolio choice frameworks that are available to help guide this choice. The one we find the most helpful is from the *Journal of Business Strategy*, adapted by Professor Arnoldo C. Hax from Ian C. MacMillan's article 'Seizing Competitive Initiative'.

The two dimensions that he uses based on which to prioritize business segments are: (a) the attractiveness of the business segment and (b) the internal competitive strength of the company (internal capabilities enabling a firm to serve customer needs, relative to competition). The Hax framework suggests five factors to evaluate business segment attractiveness—market factors, competitive factors, economic and government factors, technological factors and social factors, which we have discussed in Chapter 2. We believe that the CBBS approach is to think more broadly about the dimensions of evaluation in terms of *gain* (attractiveness of a business segment) and *pain* (internal capabilities that enable the firm to serve the key needs of customers,

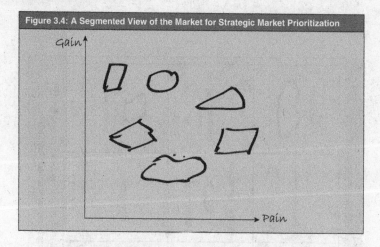

Figure 3.4: A Segmented View of the Market for Strategic Market Prioritization

relative to competition). As we have briefly discussed in Chapter 2 and will discuss further in subsequent chapters, including as many *customer world* variables in the assessment of gain and pain makes the strategic market choices far more robust.

A *build aggressively* business segment (shown as a in Figure 3.5) is usually one for which a company would want to invest and own assets on the ground. A typical *prove viability* candidate business (depicted with an oval in the diagram) is one where lots of opportunity exists *out there*, but the company has no inherent strength or capability as yet to exploit it. For example, if Mahindra & Mahindra were to think about the rural consumer whom they serve with farm equipment, and look at rural education as an opportunity given the rural demand–supply gap for quality education, it would be a classic *prove viability* business. Pilot locations and small pilot projects that enable the company to understand the challenges in offering a competitively sound product

Figure 3.5: The Strategy Concept and Process

Attractiveness of business segment: GAIN			
High	Build aggressively Build gradually	Build selectively	Prove viability
Medium	Maintain aggressively Maintain selectively	Maintain aggressively Maintain selectively	Competitive harasser
Low	Maintain aggressively Maintain selectively	Prove viability	Divest: Liquidate
	High	Medium	Low

Internal competitive strength (internal capabilities enabling firm to serve key customer needs, relative to competition): PAIN

Source: Adapted from Hax and Majluf (1995).

and a socially responsible business proposition would be the way to proceed in such a case.

In a subsequent chapter dedicated to this *where* to compete decision, we will discuss in detail (a) how to identify business segments that are stable and create competitive advantage through the manner in which the segmentation is done and (b) how to evaluate *pain* and *gain* of different business-market segments using criteria drawn from the world of consumers and not from the supply side alone.

3. **Having decided *where* or which parts or business segments of the market to compete in with what intensity, the next issue that a business-market strategy must address is: for each chosen *where*, *how* should the business play or compete to win?** Using a games analogy, the *where to compete* is about deciding whether to play cricket or hockey or kabaddi and with what relative intensity. If cricket, whether 20–20 or test? For 20–20 cricket, the question then is, *how* can this company

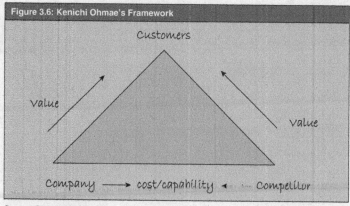

Figure 3.6: Kenichi Ohmae's Framework

Source: Ohmae (1991).

play in order to win? New kind of bowling moves or XYZ-type batting? And so on. The Kenichi Ohmae framework that we discussed in Chapter 2 (see Figure 3.6) is the essence of deciding *how to compete*.

The task is to find ways by which the company can deliver superior value than competitors, to customers that it wants to serve, or, where it has chosen to compete; and to be able to deliver this superior value through a capability or a cost advantage compared to competition.

As we explained earlier, the engine or the *front end*, or the hero of our CBBS approach to business strategy is the business-market strategy. How this strategy gets developed constitutes a significant portion of this book. We hope we have clearly distinguished this from the functional marketing strategy by now and delineated its contours.

CHAPTER 4

The Where to Compete Decision

The first leg of the business-market strategy, the front end of the business strategy is to decide strategic market priorities for the business, i.e., identify which parts of the market a business chooses to participate in (or compete in or play in) and which parts it will not compete/play/participate in; and within those chosen parts of the market (that is, the playgrounds of its choice), how hard—with what effort, energy, and resources—will it play?

The underlying logic of the *where to compete* decision is an acceptance that what is termed 'the market' (for example, the car market, the container-shipping market, the passenger air traffic market) is actually not a single homogeneous entity. Rather, it is a collection of heterogeneous parts or sub-markets or market segments, each with its own special characteristics (for example, office fleet car market and individual-owned car market, discount holiday fliers and business class business fliers, etc.). This then leads logically to an acceptance of the fact that some of these sub-markets can be more attractive and more necessary for a company to participate in than the others. Hence, companies need to

73

Figure 4.1: The CBBS Framework: WHERE to Compete

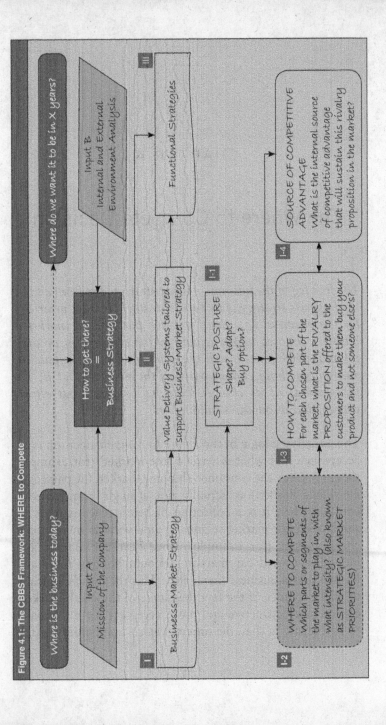

prioritize the extent and nature of their participation in each part of the market (sub-market). They need to do this by examining the long- and short-term attractiveness of each sub-market and explicitly deciding what the strategic value and importance of each is in aiding the company to achieve its goals.

This process, commonly referred to by business and market strategists as 'strategic market prioritization', is necessary for two reasons:

1. Resources, efforts, and organizational energy are not unlimited.

   Hence, market segmentation and prioritization is an efficient and effective way to use them for maximum returns.
2. Different parts of the market have different requirements for success, and need different business games (or business models).

   Not explicitly recognizing sub-markets and not prioritizing them makes companies either attempt to play a multitude of games in the market and end up with suboptimal results in all, or attempt to serve the entire market with just a single *one-size-fits-all* game, which makes the business vulnerable to competitors who either customize for or specialize in certain sub-markets.

In this chapter we discuss:

- What business actions follow as a result of implementing strategic market prioritization?
- How to actually define sub-markets or market segments in order to make the *where to compete* decision?

- How best to arrive at strategic market prioritization of sub-markets (also referred to in the rest of this chapter as business-market segments to emphasize the fact that this market segmentation is done for the purposes of business strategy and not for functional marketing strategy).

ARTICULATING STRATEGIC MARKET PRIORITIES AND BUSINESS ACTIONS THAT RESULT FROM THEM

In the previous chapters, we discussed different ways of articulating the strategic value, hence the strategic priority, of a business-market segment. The Boston Consulting Group (BCG) framework of cash cows (must give more milk than it consumes food) and stars (must be fed aggressively and grown so that they can shine brighter) and question marks (fund them with care, measure their returns carefully and do not give them the benefit of the doubt) is one way of articulating this. The Hax framework of *build aggressively*, *maintain selectively*, *prove viability*, etc., that we discussed in Chapter 3, is another way of articulating the strategic priority of each sub-market or business-market segment.

Some businesses define intensity of play in a relative sense. A typical example of this would read something like this:

Our main priority is to focus on staying the market leader in the toothpaste and white toothpowder part of the oral care market, aggressively driving its growth since India is still an under penetrated market for these. (Read this as: The priority of this part of the market is so high that the CEO gets the sack if there is any slippage in market share or growth targets.)

76

OR:

In the toothbrushes and non-white toothpowder parts of the oral care market, we will build selectively, in progressive geographies where upgradation to better oral care products is happening at a fast pace. In the rest of the oral care market we will maintain a strong presence but not invest beyond a minimum prescribed level. (Read this as: Let us have new brand managers cut their teeth on the non-priority geographies of toothbrush and non-white toothpowder markets; if any local competitor starts aggressive marketing or price cutting, do not respond. Just refresh the pack graphics and tighten screws on loyal distributors!) Equally understood is that if even a small, tentative *dip-toe-and-test-the-waters* attempt is made by any new competition in the toothpastes and white toothpowders market, then all barrels will be fired in order to destroy it even before it gains a toe hold.

Sometimes businesses choose not to play in certain market segments even if they are growing at a fast clip; for example, low-price airlines, the sub-100 cc motorcycle or in the voice services BPO market, because they feel that their cost position will not allow them to make a profit, or that the risk of de-focusing the organization would be too great. The sad part is that they still calculate their market share based on the total market size, rather than just the part of the market that they have chosen to play in, and take panic-driven desperate measures to retain their market share—like price discounting in their core market. And sometimes organizations do just the reverse and do not make such explicit *where not to compete* choices (they go wherever competitors are going or wherever growth is taking place) that result in very bad experiences and significant financial damages, not to mention effects on their main business as well.

It is not always necessary or obvious that companies should choose *not* to compete in unattractive parts of the market. For example, it often happens that businesses explicitly choose to play in unattractive, commoditized, crowded market segments (sub-markets) because these are bulk builders that keep the distribution channel happy or serve the purpose of tying up the working capital of distribution channels that could otherwise be used to stock the products of the competitors. It is also possible that companies choose to participate in currently small sub-markets with slow growth because they are large in other geographies or more developed markets and, hence, building a *ready-to-scale* but small presence in the former is a good bet to place.

IDENTIFICATION OF SUB-MARKETS (BUSINESS-MARKET SEGMENTS) FOR THE PURPOSE OF STRATEGIC MARKET PRIORITIZATION

Most strategy developers or companies pay the least amount of attention to identifying sub-markets for the purpose of determining which parts of the market to focus on. They work with standard industry definitions of sub-markets, which are usually based on product descriptions (A–B–C category cars, 40/25/30 HP tractors, glucose biscuits, cream biscuits, etc.).

Quite often, they also define sub-markets in terms of competitor territories (unorganized sector or grey market/ users of Company X) or even price points (mid-price segments of the market) or technologies (CDMA segment of the market versus GSM segment). Normally, at the level of developing business strategy, we do not find too many customer-based definitions of sub-markets. At best, strategic market prioritization is done at the broad level of *mass market, consuming class* (which could mean anything and anybody with any need) or 'bottom of the pyramid' (BOP) consumers, etc. But we believe that great strategic value can come from enlightened identification of sub-markets, which offer greater strategic value to the business. This is the whole purpose of business-market segmentation (that is, of identifying, defining and prioritizing sub-markets and serving them with customized offerings). Therefore, cookie cutter, standard industry definitions of segments, or sub-markets is not good enough. They are merely classification variables, not methods of identifying parts of the market that companies should own or concede in order to build stable, sustainable positions in the market in line with their goals, capabilities and constraints.

Second, we believe that markets are not made up of a collection of product types or competitors' businesses or technologies. Markets are made up of customers or people who have needs that a business is looking to fulfil, and there is an economic exchange in the process—one buys, the other sells. The purpose of a business-market strategy is to define which of these people and needs a company should go after (or not), in order to build a sustainable, stable business.

Therefore, we believe that the key to a *where to compete* decision lies in the first step of market segmentation or identifying sub-markets such that: *(a)* the identification provides a basis for competitive advantage by the very way in which it has been defined; and *(b)* it is customer-based and, hence, as explained in earlier chapters, is more stable over time, and is totally focused on the entity that pays for the revenue of the company and drives the cost structure to a certain extent!

DEFINING SUB-MARKETS (BUSINESS-MARKET SEGMENTS) FOR COMPETITIVE ADVANTAGE

The task at hand is to identify sub-markets (or market segments) that are especially advantageous to a company and are hard for competitors to serve. Actually, we feel that the word *identify* is too tame for what this process involves. The task actually is to *unearth* or *carve out*, *skillfully*. For example, consider a company like Maruti Suzuki Ltd, which has the widest service network in terms of geographic spread, and the lion's share of the population of cars in the market today by virtue of being the only 'new age' car company in the land of old models of Indian cars for several years before other competitors entered India. Maruti's high-priority sub-markets, which would yield competitive advantage, would be Maruti owners or individuals in or from Maruti-owning families wanting to replace their Maruti cars or buy another car. Another high-priority sub-market would be car buyers in geographically far-flung areas given the head-start it has over competition in building its distribution service network. If, however, the Maruti product strategy and the product offerings are not in tune with the heads of these market segments that offer the best strategic value, then the hunt for competitively advantageous sub-markets has to continue. For example, if existing Maruti car owners, at the peak of Maruti's share of the car population in India, wanted to *upgrade* to higher features and performance models, where Maruti did not offer products or where competitors offered far better products, then targeting the segment of Maruti owners planning to replace their cars offers no strategic advantage. Assuming that Maruti has just one model—a small car with a low price-performance point, the popular mistake assumption would be to equate the entry-level product with the entry-level customer, i.e., the first-time car buyer.

However, first-time car buyers, called 'entry-level customers', need not be small car or 'entry-level product' buyers. They could be rich young executives entering the car market for the first time, who want and can afford a car at a far-higher price-performance point than Maruti products offer. If Maruti is able to offer only its basic model, then, in order to gain competitive advantage, it would have to identify segments in the market in a totally different way—people who want a car, but cannot afford to pay more and are willing to settle for less, and whose value comes from just the act of having four wheels instead of no wheels or two wheels.

As we will show in subsequent chapters as well, and as we have described in our framework, a CBBS approach would start with first looking at the opportunities offered by the consumer environment that are advantageous to the company to achieve its goals and then designing or aligning products to these customer opportunities. However, we also recognize that the real world of business is not a perfect world and sometimes the products come first and are hard to change. But even in such situations, as we have just discussed in the Maruti example, the discipline of searching for customer-based segments that provide competitive advantage for the company remains a critical element of business-market strategy—which, in turn, is a critical element of business strategy.

To close out this thought with another example: The Indian arm of a global market leader company supplying anything B2B, be it advertising or polyurethane, would find competitively advantageous sub-markets in customers who place a lot of value on the *global* expertise and *global* relationships of this supplier company. In the case of polyurethane, these customer segments could be large Liquefied Natural Gas (LNG) pipeline-type projects with international consultants and global consortia involved, or even small Indian footwear exporters who supply to reputed international retail chains, global car manufacturers who re-create locally their global supply chain and vendors and so on. The paradigm here would be to monetize the *global* element of the company's capability through appropriate identification of market segments.

Companies worry and struggle a lot to achieve business differentiation, to stand apart in a uniform sea of competitors who, like them, look alike, sound alike, do alike and price alike. The thought we want to plant here is that *business differentiation can come not just from what you specifically offer and how (that is, from your talk and walk), but even more fundamentally from how differently you segment your market.* Business strategies based on a unique scheme of market segmentation could result in highly differentiated business as well.

A study we saw several years ago for an international confectionery company showed that they thought about their business segments in terms of the life stage of their consumers and needs with respect to confectionery that came from each life stage. Thus, the very young children below six years wanted edible toys like whistle sweets (Business Segment 1), the slightly older seven-to-twelve-year-olds wanted the best sweet bulk for their limited pocket money (Business Segment 2), the teens wanted to show they were different from the kids and growing up, they just started dating, and wanted more experimental tastes and forms which were more distinctive, like honey and nougatine chocolate bars (Business Segment 3), and the young adults wanted to consume confectionery with sophisticated adult tastes and in forms that were not guilt-inducing (Business Segment 4). Each of these then resulted in a sharply differentiated product portfolio and pricing and branding strategies compared to the competition. The dominant logic of how the company thought about the market was very different.

DEFINING SUB-MARKETS (BUSINESS-MARKET SEGMENTS) BASED ON CUSTOMER VARIABLES, NOT SUPPLY-SIDE VARIABLES

The purpose of a business-market strategy is to define playgrounds and games that a company can discover and dominate ahead of competition and defend from imitators— or if not dominate, at least get a decent slice of and hold on to despite efforts from competitors. Our view, stated repeatedly in this book, is that for Customer-Based Business, companies must, right at the highest level of business strategy development, define these playgrounds (sub-markets or market segments) using customer variables rather than supply-side variables. Therefore, shifting product boundaries bringing new sources of competition, despite new competitor initiatives, will not make the strategy obsolete or irrelevant but it will remain relevant and defensible.

Interestingly, even though many companies define and work with customer-based market segments at the level of functional marketing strategies, for the purpose of business strategy development, they define market segments in terms of supply-side variables—product segments or competitor franchises or technology-based segments.

South West Airlines is the poster child of business strategy, strategic differentiation and winning from it in the most exemplary way. The core of SWA's business strategy came from customer-based market segmentation. They looked at the market not as airline customers, or type of airline services or any such supply-centric definitions. Their strategic advantage came from looking at people (all possible customers) and their travel needs and identifying a sub-market of regular, short haul, road travellers that they thought they could serve better by designing an air service that would decrease door-to-door travelling time, match cost and make the whole trip a lot more fun than driving by car; and most important, by managing to do it all at a cost that generated a profit for the airline.

To take another example, as long as we think of the coffee market as being divided into sub-markets like filter and instant or chicory blended versus pure Colombian, we lose the plot in terms of designing or business strategy that can provide long-term strategic advantage. When we move away from product-based definitions of sub-markets to customer based definitions, as in 'why do you drink a particular cup of coffee', the sub-markets that emerge could be *relaxation, stimulation* and *social networking facilitation*. If we think of each of these as a market itself (the same way we think of Europe, America and China as markets in themselves), then we can see that the way we build businesses for each would be quite different. The *business model* for the *relaxation* market could be café-centred as could the model for *social networking*, but these would be very different paradigms. Then, perhaps, the centrepiece of the 'stimulation' market could be product offers based on grades of caffeine delivered through vending machines in offices, airports, bus stations, etc., and other public places where people stay late; and offering far better 'takeaway' packaging so that on-the-go can be really easy. Thinking this way opens up several new avenues for differentiation and competitive advantage.

The IT sector in India defines its sub-markets or business-market segments in product terms—application development, maintenance, system integration, Enterprise Resource Planning (ERP) implementation, business consulting or IT-led business transformation. They further divide application development (customized software development) into verticals that customers belong to (retail, automotive, etc.) and into geographies (Europe, Africa, etc.). The only problem with this scheme of business-market segmentation is that the sub-markets derived using this approach may not be either homogeneous in terms of customer needs, nor competitively advantageous for the business. While it is true that retail sector customers are different in their IT needs from automotive sector customers and European customers are different in their approach to vendor selection from US businesses, there is still no fundamental homogeneity between them in terms of *customer benefits,* on the back of which business advantage can be built.

Such business-market segmentation is like saying 'we offer large shoes to men with big feet or small shoes to those with small feet' (that is, retail sector relevant solutions to retail sector companies and automotive sector relevant solutions to auto sector companies). There is no big deal to that at all; no great story or business advantage in that. It is like table stakes that you have to put down on the table at the start of a poker game in order to qualify to enter the game! McDonald's is not practicing superior business-market segmentation by saying 'no beef burgers' in largely Hindu countries and 'no pork fat used for cooking' in largely Islamic countries!

A customer-centred way to look at business-market segmentation for an IT company is to think about what customers want from IT and how they think about the benefits of IT. Ade McCormack, a columnist in the *Financial Times*, in the 14 May 2007 issue of the paper talks of 'four budgetary pots' that companies think about their IT needs in. The pots are 'run the business', 'grow the business', 'change the business' and 'save the business'. In 'run the business', the focus is on supporting day-to-day operations. The IT function is to ensure that the 'lights stay on'. Indian IT companies tend to think about this in terms of 'maintenance' (product centrically) and lose out on the idea. While maintenance is a part of 'run the business IT', it is not all of it. There is scope for value enhancement and new offers here that companies like IBM pioneer. They take over IT assets and people to provide 'run the business' services, etc. In 'grow the business IT', McCormack talks of how the context is that 'the business is taking on more and more customers and expanding geographies and the job of the IT function is to provide a scalable platform for growth.' In 'change the business IT', the context described is that of a big-ship-like company being in waters infested by 'smaller, younger, hungrier and more agile competitors. Options come down to sinking the ship or changing the business. The IT function needs to explore the use of innovative technologies to redefine the business model'. And finally, in 'save the business IT', as McCormack so lucidly describes it, the organization has 'become flabby' because of too much of the good times and 'a corporate coronary [that] awaits. . . . The IT function needs to guide the business as a whole, to improve efficiency.'

It is, thus, intuitively and analytically obvious that identifying sub-markets (or strategic business-market segmentation) for an IT services company based on the customer worldview of 'what problem do I deal with in my company and what is the role of IT', is far superior to an inner-focused worldview of 'what services do I provide and what table stakes do I build into it'. Systems Integration or ERP implementation could be a part of any of these and come with different price tags and totally different 'scope of work' delineation.

Another article by Alan Lane in the same issue of the *Financial Times* quotes an Accenture Survey of Small and Medium Enterprises (SMEs) and identifies interesting sub-markets of superior value or where competitive advantage can be built. First, the entire 'SME companies' space is an interesting sub-market for ERP-related businesses because they are crying out for productivity and efficiency improvement and the existing range of ERP services and software have been traditionally configured for large companies—and have a high cost and high degrees of company-level customization. The article makes the point that there is a market opportunity where 'the trick is . . . to rewrite sophisticated systems' to make them more suitable (and more affordable) for smaller companies. The trick also is to do only that amount of customization that makes a critical difference to their business. Second, industries such as fashion and those using farm-originated raw material have special needs and would pay for features that support these needs, and, hence, form valuable market segments for businesses to focus on. Third, the Accenture survey the article quotes also makes the point that ERP is underutilized in several companies and close to half say that if they had a training budget, they could use the solution better. Therefore, business-market segment could also be defined in terms of customer variables like amount spent on

ERP solution and level of utilization that could cut across industry verticals.

For example, one of the axes along which Nokia thinks of its business-market segments is based on customer needs, as gleaned from how customers think about their cell phone; and it excels at designing the product range that delivers against each of these needs. Its sub-markets are people who think of their cell phone primarily as a means of entertainment, or as a fashion accessory, or as a productivity tool or as what they label as 'premium'—people who know they have arrived and see these as gifts or *perks* of arrivals.

We know of a travel agency whose main line of business is organizing holidays. They think of their business-market segments as those who are 'money-rich and time-poor', and those who are 'time-rich and money-poor'. For the latter, they have a web-based business and for the former, personalized services of a holiday planner.

Subsequent chapters will discuss in greater detail several examples of business-market segmentation and how companies actually arrive at them. In this chapter, we would primarily discuss the conceptual framework.

PRIORITIZING SUB-MARKETS: FRAMEWORK FOR CHOICE

Having separated the market into its various distinctive component sub-markets or business-market segments, the next step is to actually prioritize them and choose the sub-markets in which the business should play, and the intensity with which it should play. In Chapter 3, we suggested that the prioritization should be done along two broad dimensions—what is the *gain* offered by the segment and what is the *pain* needed in order to realize the gain. Traditional business strategy language often labels these dimensions as 'industry attractiveness' and 'competitiveness', and uses supply-side variables to measure both. We suggest, to begin with, that the dimensions be labelled 'market attractiveness' and 'ability to compete to win'.

MARKET ATTRACTIVENESS

Using the term 'market attractiveness' instead of 'industry attractiveness' leads us to acknowledge that markets are collections of customers with intrinsic characteristics rather than a collection of suppliers with P&L statements. The notion that market attractiveness is determined by the turnover and profit and growth trajectories of existing players in the markets rests on the assumption that existing players have done everything that needs to be done to make the market into the size and profitability that it presently is. Yet, strategy books are replete with examples of how some company discovered a different market (customer segment or need space) and ended up creating a new market space that was far more profitable or larger than its competitors.

Honda created a new market in the USA selling 100 cc bikes with profitability and size quite different from Harley Davidson; Nirma defined a new market for detergents comprising laundry soap targeted at lower-income consumers, and created a different picture of *industry attractiveness*; SWA created a totally different market with much greater attractiveness than the traditional airline industry and so on. In order to get a fair assessment of the attractiveness of a market or a market segment, we recommend analysing its attractiveness from both the supplier- and the customer- based perspectives.

Typical supply-side analyses of industry attractiveness look at Structure–Conduct–Performance-type analyses to determine industry attractiveness (what structure of market share, what conduct is typically exhibited by current players and what is their financial performance). We suggest that a similar analysis of market attractiveness be done from the customer perspective: the structure of customer demand, conduct and concerns of customers and their satisfaction level with available options. Detailed examples to illustrate this will be given in a later chapter on analytics, Chapter 9.

Typical supply-side analyses of market attractiveness looks at sales and sales growth of the service or product widget that is defined as being 'the market'—perhaps sub-divided into sales by a sub-type of widget (150 cc bike, step-through scooter, discount segment airline sales versus mainstreams segment airlines sales, etc.). We suggest customer-based market attractiveness assessment based on the number of people with high intensity need or desire for something, their past and likely future growth, their ability to spend and likelihood of income and expenditure growths in the future, and so on. To return to the SWA example, market attractiveness assessed based on the airline industry's sales, growth and profitability would have pointed to a verdict of lower attractiveness than looking at it from a customer-based perspective—the attractiveness of large groups of mid-level, short-haul, point-to-point business travellers (like salesmen on regular beats) who drive and are looking for a faster though not costlier means of transport.

The market attractiveness for instant blood-glucose monitoring machines for individual use is low in India when viewed from the supply side. But from a customer-based perspective, this is definitely an attractive market—a very large and growing number of diabetics in a country just starting to consume and getting urbanized in lifestyle favourable occupation demographics (large numbers of self-employed people who recognize the need to stay fit to earn a living) and no form of health care or social security, with very active advertising by sugar substitutes. Similarly, the small tractor (<25 HP) segment of the Indian tractor market is unattractive in terms of historical sales and growth, but the enormous number of small farms in India, their increasing incomes and their diversifying into cash crops and non-farm activities, point to a very attractive market of helping small farmers who want to mechanize. The mismatch between 'industry' attractiveness and 'customer-based business' attractiveness is usually because no supplier has developed a business offering that offers affordable and accessible ways to cater to customers' needs and attitudes, and yet profit from it.

COMPETITIVENESS (ABILITY TO COMPETE TO WIN)

We suggest that competitiveness should be assessed on whether the company in question can do better than competitors on dimensions that customers value. It is about assessing the ability of the company to compete to win.

Traditional business strategy analysis usually deals with competitiveness as benchmarking the insides of one company with another. It is about whether the company has an ability to perform better than the competition on those dimensions that customers use to make choices.

Our clients often ask us whether the *ability to compete* dimension used to prioritize strategic market segments should be based on what the company can do today or what it could potentially do in the future. They argue that if it is what capability a company can potentially acquire to compete in the future, then all companies should be equally competitive.

Our view is that an assessment of a company's current capability to serve a market vis-à-vis its competitors' ability to do the same is one data point that is definitely needed. However, the other data point needed is: over what time frame and at what costs can it acquire the required new capabilities at a minimum acceptable level to help it win in the market. If an immediate acquisition can improve a company's ability to compete in a market or sub-market, then the *pain* of serving that market is determined by the cost of the acquisition and perhaps the time taken to integrate it with the current business (if that is needed to serve the market well).

Further, if there is a very attractive business-market segment in which a company's present ability to compete is poor and its ability to acquire capabilities to compete in the future comes at a high cost and a certain amount of time, then, going back to the Hax framework for market prioritization (as in Chapter 3), this would be a segment that should be accorded a priority of 'prove viability'. It would not be a 'build aggressively' candidate market. A classic example of this is when a modern format jewellery store chain business says that the Indian market for gold ornaments made for weddings is worth Rs 40,000 crore, is quite recession-proof and definitely slated to grow, but the family jeweller reigns supreme in this market and has the ability to offer generational continuity and memory sell at daily gold prices and not 'per finished piece' standard price and manage his inventory valuation, which a retailer like itself cannot, this is definitely a 'prove viability' candidate market even if the total size of the pie is Rs 40,000 crore and it is growing at the rate of 15 per cent per year.

SUMMARY

In this chapter we have discussed the conceptual ideas behind the *where to compete* decision that forms the first element of a business-market strategy. We also, rather colloquially, think of the *where to compete* decision as 'what game, which playgrounds?' Will the company be playing cricket or hockey or its own combination game of 'crockey'? At Lords? In Wimbledon? Or, on the streets of Mumbai on a Sunday? (See I.2 in Figure 4.1.)

And if it has several games or playgrounds, which one will it assign its prime resources to, and which one will it pay a lot less attention to? We believe that getting business-market segmentation right (i.e., capable of creating strategic value, competitive advantage and using customer-based variables) is a very major part of getting the overall strategy right.

CHAPTER 5

The How to Compete Decision

Once the business arenas have been prioritized at the corporate strategy level, and the sub-markets chosen within each business arena and prioritized, the next step is to actually decide how to play in each sub-market in order to win. See I.3 in Figure 5.1.

Winning in a chosen market space means winning over customers—getting them to choose to stay with your company, to pay the price that they can afford and that makes you profitable. Obviously, in the act of choosing your company, customers express a preference for your company over other competing offers that they could potentially choose. We often have clients interrupt us at this step and say: 'But we do not have any competition—we are the only widget of this kind in the market.' Our answer is simple: 'Your competition, in this case, is the traditional way of fulfilling the need, or the customer's choice to do nothing at all to satisfy the need.' So, the 'competition' faced by a seller of oral rehydration salts for treatment of diarrhoea could be in the form of the customer's decision to do nothing at all, but just live with the problem and let nature take its course. Or, 'competition' to an answering machine is a maid or a

Figure 5.1: The CBBS Framework: How to Compete

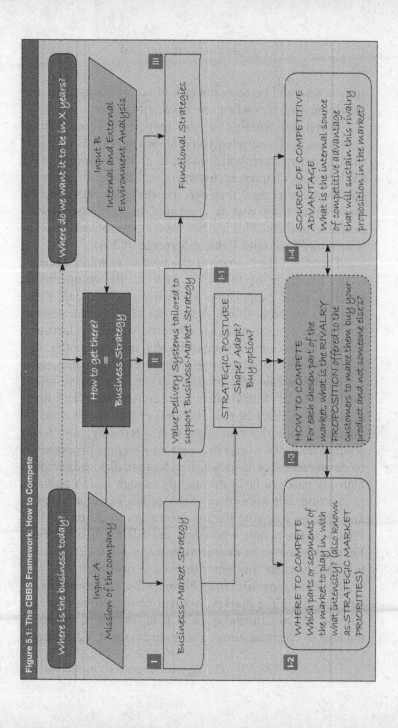

spouse who will perform the task of taking phone calls and recording messages when one is away from home.

Therefore, winning in the market is about getting customers to choose what you offer *instead* of other options that they may have (which includes *doing nothing*). As we explained in Chapter 3, customers will choose to buy your company's offering if they perceive that they are obtaining more value from you as compared to any other option available to them. This is what we will, henceforth, label as 'Consumer/Customer Value Advantage' (CVA).

Therefore, the essence of the *how to compete* decision is the designing of this CVA, that is, the competitively superior value proposition for customers. We call it the *why buy me* proposition. Again, our clients often need to be prodded to recognize that while individual products and services have a *why buy me* embedded into every offer, it is equally necessary to have one at the level of the company as a whole. For example, *problem-solving innovation* lies at the heart of all Philips' offers to its consumers, which helps to make their lives better. The kind of innovation done by Philips is quite different from that offered by, say, Sony, and hence, the two offer different *why buy me* propositions to consumers. For instance, if a football field adjoining a highway needs to be lit up brightly enough for TV cameras to function, but without any light spilling onto the highway and causing a driving hazard, customers ought to think of Philips as the people who could provide the best solution. Philips, in turn, must deliver its *problem-solving innovation* in a situation like this better than its competitors!

Similarly, any offer from Nirma will certainly not be the best quality in the market, but will be of adequate quality and be priced affordably. The company does, however, manage to create customer value advantage (CVA) as compared to the higher-quality–higher-priced offerings of its competitors for a certain segment of customers.

Business strategy documents often do not provide explicit and clear answers to this most fundamental question: Why should customers buy from your company? When pushed to answer this question, many of our clients say: 'Customers should buy from my company *because we have superior manufacturing/technology/product design*/talent, etc.' If they are the product trailblazers in the market, then they reply by saying: 'Customers should buy me because this is modern, advanced, easy, etc.' If they are the old established market leaders, then their answer is: 'Customers should buy from my company because we offer good quality/trust/ distribution/market leadership, etc.' The first set of answers is all about 'look at me, see how wonderful I am', and begs the question, 'What do customers gain as a result of this?' The second set of answers is at least customer-centred in that they answer the question of: 'What do I offer to customers that should be the reason for them to buy me?' However, quality, trust, fair business practices, care, and distribution are probably what most of the companies from the same peer group are offering in the market. In fact, in many mature markets with several high-quality competitors, as in the case of automotive or pharmaceuticals or biscuits, these become the hygiene factors—the basic set of reasons that need to exist in order to even form a part of the customer's consideration set.

The 'why should customers buy from me' question is actually only one part of the question. The entire question should read: 'Why should customers buy me and not somebody else/something else?' Therefore, we prefer to call this not just a value proposition (to the customer), but also a rivalry proposition. Calling it this, we find, forces businesses to think more sharply about why they are better, not just why they are good, forcing them to articulate it in terms of what does it do for the customer.

The rivalry proposition is, to belabour the point again, (a) the competitively superior value proposition; (b) for the business as a whole; and (c) articulated in terms of what value the customer receives. Several times, to our dismay, we find that advertising tag lines are viewed as synonymous with rivalry propositions. However, rivalry propositions relate to the core competence of the company. C.K. Prahalad likens a corporation to a tree. The branches are business units, and the buds, flowers and fruits are individual products and services. The root system that nourishes all the parts of the tree is the core competence of the company, that is, something which the company does very well. The rivalry proposition to the customer is the answer to the question 'Why buy me and no one else?' It contains the compelling benefits that are on offer, which, ideally, are as a result of the deployment of the core competence. To go back to Ohmae's strategic triangle that we discussed in Chapter 3 (see Figure 5.2), creating the CVA is about figuring out how the value delivered to the customer by your company is better than that delivered by the competitor and sustainable by virtue of some real advantages that your business has over its competitors in terms of capability and/or cost.

Thus, a snack food company that says its rivalry proposition is *indulgence in taste + healthier alternative* to other options must have the capability to make *good for you* baked corn chips and high-fibre biscuits that taste as good as fried potato chips and refined flour and sugar biscuits, or

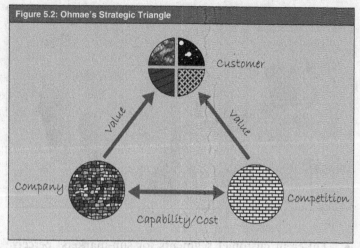

Figure 5.2: Ohmae's Strategic Triangle

Source: Adapted from Ohmae (1991).

Note: Value = ∑Benefits − ∑Cost (as perceived by the consumer).

to provide less salt and cholesterol in potato chips that taste the same as the real ones, or make sugar-free chocolates that taste as good as those with sugar. Alternatively, it must have the capability to create an entirely different range of snacks that is as tasty and exciting, and completely non-comparable to the existing options.

Key points in Ohmae's strategic triangle—the key framework for thinking about rivalry propositions:

- Value advantage must be perceived by customers—otherwise it is no advantage at all. Whether customers perceive the value on their own or are taught to perceive it by the company is a matter of how to do so. The principal point is that the customer must perceive it in one way or the other. So CVA is actually CPVA.

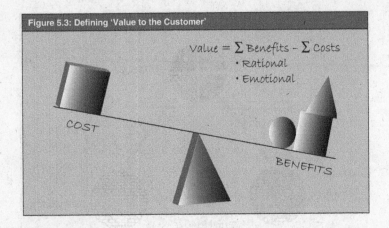

Figure 5.3: Defining 'Value to the Customer'

- Different customer segments (or sub-markets) perceive value from the same product offer differently, as the long-standing, multi-country HSBC campaign shows so evocatively, one man's meat is another man's poison; one man's 'cool' is another person's 'shabby'.
- Customer perceived value advantage (CPVA) and rivalry proposition are strategically more sound and precise concepts than customer value proposition. Better than the competition has to be a central theme.
- Many strategists use the phrase competitive advantage. We recommend the phrase customer perceived value advantage over competition, because it forces customer-centric thinking.

So what exactly is this construct or the concept of 'value to the customer'? We find that the word 'value' is used in many different ways to mean different things. Therefore, the next section of this chapter will discuss our concept and construct of *value to the customer*.

UNDERSTANDING CUSTOMER PERCEIVED VALUE

Value proposition is a catch-all phrase extensively used (and abused) in day-to-day business conversations. In the heady days of the dotcom boom, we have even heard it being used to describe what the likely financial value of the enterprise could be! In this section, we will state clearly the definition of 'value' that we use. We will discuss methodology to determine what consumer perceived value is in later chapters.

The definition of value is best encapsulated in the following equation:

Value = Benefit − Cost (V = B − C)

The model we work with is that every consumer has a computer inside his head. He sees every offer as having a set of benefits that add some units of value to him and a set of costs that detract from the units of value added by the benefits. The net value of benefits and costs is the perceived value of the offer to the customer. Customers choose between competing offers by selecting the one that has the maximum perceived value.

We have repeatedly cautioned that 'value' is as perceived by customers, and not as perceived by the suppliers themselves. So how do customers process value to arrive at the units of value that Offer A or B provides? We think about approaching it this way: each customer's computer has a value processing algorithm of its own. This algorithm defines how much the consumer values what benefits and how steep he considers the costs (the assumption is that in a sub-market or consumer segment, the value processing algorithm inside the heads of all people in that segment is similar). Using this algorithm, they evaluate all the benefits and the costs that they see/notice/find for each offer, sum them up, and arrive at a net value score.

Using mathematical notations:

Net value of offer A = Σ value obtained from each benefit of offer A
$- \Sigma$ value detracted by each cost of offer B.

Customers will compare the net value of Offers A, B, and C, and pick the one that has the highest net value (see Figure 5.3).

The purpose of a rivalry proposition, therefore, is to ensure that Value from Me > Value from Competitors, as customers process and perceive value.

It is important to note certain things about consumer value processing.

1. *Cost is not price.* It is the total cost of usage calculated in the way the customer thinks about it.
- *Variables along which cost is processed are defined by customers:* All too often, companies look at costs based on their own cost processing models and then say the customers are wrong when they say *it costs too much*!

    In the customer's mind, cost could even be related to the eventual re-sale or trade-in price of a gadget if the customer considers that relevant. For instance, in case of processed foods that serve as convenient meal substitutes, Indian consumers think of *cost per full stomach for a family of four*. With the increase in borrowing to fund durables, absolute price ceased to be processed as price and came to be seen in terms of the monthly EMIs to be paid. So, a difference of Rs 5000 in price between two otherwise similar competitive offers might result in a difference of, say, 100 units of value, whereas the difference between their EMIs could be as low as Rs 50 per month and not be consequential at all or be just 10 units of value apart. When customers think about cost, they also include the cost of re-training employees to use a particular software or machinery or the cost of getting vendors aligned with it. Some customers think about cost in terms of the lifetime cost of usage (including wear and tear) or include the extra spare parts inventory that needs to be carried because of the limited spares distribution network that a company has. Buyers of air conditioners or two-wheelers in India attach a far higher weightage to the *running costs* (the cost of electricity or petrol consumed) than the one-time purchase price of the unit. Yet manufacturers or marketers continue to fight price wars, expending far more energy in bringing manufacturing costs down, even though the final reduction in price achieved often does not make any real impact on customer perceived value.

Distribution and franchising strategies are often built on *model financials* constructed by the MBA whiz-kid in the office and are quite different from the way retailers process their cost of operations and the returns that they expect. Exactly the same happens in the case of marketing farm inputs to farmers. Very often, the case is not that they doubt the benefit they will receive from the offer—it is just that the factors that they use to process cost is different.

- *Costs can be real costs or probability of incurring the cost:* When consumers look at buying a smuggled or fake brand or a store brand appliance with the ubiquitous 'Made in China' tag, they not only look at the low price tag, but also add on the probable loss (if the piece in question ends up being of poor quality), thereby requiring it to be replaced in perhaps less than a week. On the other hand, if the retailer is a known one, the customer might attach a lower probability to receiving a bad-quality item and be willing to pay more for it. Hence, retailers selling the same goods at higher prices than their neighbours might end up more successful because in the customers' perception, the total cost of the higher priced item ends up being lower than the total cost of a similar item with lower price.

In the case of a B2B business, while buying mission-critical appliances or machines, the consumer adds probabilistic cost (expected value) of downtime to the price tag when processing cost. This in turn is based on the probability of breakdown, which, again, is based on usage or abuse specific to the customer, the customers' perceived faith in the supplier, and on the perceived speed with which breakdowns can be set right.

- *Though obvious, often very little attention is paid to the fact that different customer segments process price or cost differently:* The most obvious example is that of customers at different income levels. For the poor, an affordable *unit price* has far more value than the price/ millilitre. Hence, sachets are a win–win proposition for both the supplier and the customer. Rich consumers never know the price and weight of many of the grocery list items that they buy. They just manage at the level of the total bill for all their purchases. Yet another set of customers might look more closely at obviously large ticket items in their grocery list, but not worry about what they are paying for smaller items, though, collectively these could make up almost 70 per cent of the cost.

- *Customers do not read price tags the way we think they do:* Several years ago, Marketing and Research Group (MARG), a leading market research agency, had conducted a survey amongst middle-class housewives in Delhi and Chennai to see how they processed price or the cost of a toilet soap that they used. The findings were presented in a paper at the annual conference of the Market Research Society of India. Consumers were asked how they would react to a 15-paise increase in their favourite brand of soap. Their response was that since they had to keep track of the prices of a huge list of items like kerosene, green line bus tickets, children's shoes and bags—all frequently purchased items if you have young children—they did not really care if their brand of soap cost 15 paise more or less than its competitor. But different customers (whether B2B or B2C) have a reference or *standard* product specs and/ or brand for different products, against which they compare price in order to come to a judgement on whether it is *expensive, all right*, or *cheaper*.

2. As we move on to the 'benefits' side of the $V = B - C$ equation, there are some things to be noted about how customers process benefits.

- *Benefits can be rational and emotional:* People often assume that emotional benefits are factors only in case of low-tech B2C businesses like soaps and toothpastes, that the minute it gets technical (financial services) or technological (computers or telecom services), the rational benefits alone matter. Similarly, B2B businesses tend to believe that emotional benefits do not play much of a role.

However, we know this to be untrue in our personal experiences. Financial services are about trust. Computers are about how 'cool' the interface is or how the product makes us feel—Apple users, for instance, love the rivalry proposition that 'only pros and "certain" kinds of people use a Mac'. In B2B, even the most rational customer will find that a proposition like 'nobody ever got sacked for buying IBM machines very compelling'. Big investment banking deals are often closed on the basis of a handshake that may have generated a sense of 'I like the guy', or a belief that 'in a crunch he will not let me down'.

- *Sometimes emotional benefits can add more value than the rational ones:* Japanese technology that enables an increased level of horsepower (HP) in a motorcycle without a decrease in fuel efficiency was clearly a rational benefit of great perceived value when it was first introduced in the market. Today, when all motorcycles in the market offer the same power and mileage combinations, it is the emotional benefits of style, expression and user imagery that create the value advantage.

  In total parity products, where there is an excess supply of functional or performance-related benefits, value advantage is created either through breakthrough levels of *never before* functional benefits—which is rather tough to achieve—or through emotional benefits. Often, in mature markets with several high-quality competitors, the source of value advantage over competition has to be through achieving a slight increase in many functional benefits and in emotional benefits.

- *Consumers do not perceive the same level of value improvement for different stages of improvement in*

106

benefit levels. Bad to good can add a lot more customer perceived value than going from good to great, even if the quantum of increase in the benefit offered is exactly the same: More and more of some sort of benefit does not necessarily add more and more value to customers— even more so in the same proposition. If all the options available in the market are extremely trustworthy in financial services or insurance, then having a rivalry proposition of 'even more' trustworthy does not add any value to the customer.

Even a decrease in price behaves in the same way. For a certain band of price reduction for a given set of features, value keeps getting added. But if you were to offer Scotch whiskey at Rs 100 or a laptop at Rs 10,000, there would be doubts about its genuineness or its robustness, and perceived value would decline. A graph depicting how much value consumers perceive from each level of a benefit is what we call as a 'value curves' or 'value maps' (see Figure 5.4). Value curves are different for different benefits and also vary by consumer segments. Based on a mapping of the shapes of value curves for each benefit in each customer segment, companies need to decide which part of the value curve they should be operating in.

In Figure 5.4, the three value curves tell three different stories. The Facilities curve shows that, as far as customer perceived value is concerned, more and more of a benefit does not translate into better and better value perceived. Economists understand diminishing returns quite well, but marketers and strategists often tend to forget this. As we can see on some benefit dimensions like *personalized service* in a hotel or *job challenge* in the employment market, more and more of something, beyond a point, actually creates less value, at least to some customers. For example, an irate foreigner once told us that she was absolutely fed up of the sheer number of people in her hotel who were striving to 'establish a *relationship* with the customer', and bombarded her with questions about how she slept, how she felt, how her food was, why she did not try Option X and so on—evidently the hotel's understanding of value maps for such customers on the benefit dimension of *personalized service* was faulty; they did not realize that more and more personalized service, beyond a point, was turning off customers, and decreasing their value. A study we did amongst IIM graduates in order to develop a rivalry proposition for an MNC recruiter revealed that while job challenge was good up to a certain point, an extremely challenging job had less value perceived than a challenging job.

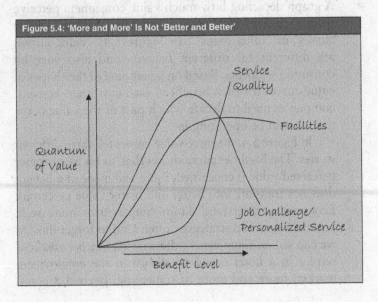

Figure 5.4: 'More and More' Is Not 'Better and Better'

The corollary to this story is that such value maps tell us that there is a *zone of benefit* in which the business needs to operate to build its rivalry proposition and that is dictated by where the competitors are operating or where the *industry* as a whole is operating. So, if the general level of service offered by the industry to customers is high, then an incremental level over this may *not* be the basis for a *rivalry* proposition even if it is an important value adding dimension for customers per se.

- *Discontinuous improvements in benefit do provide discontinuous increases in value perceived:* Innovators do radically alter the customer value processing algorithm. If every telecom company bills talk time by the minute, and a new telecom company offers to bill talk time by the second, it will add discontinuous value to poorer or very budget-conscious customers (but it may add no value to people who spend several hours on the phone!).

  Therefore, we often tell our clients that building winning rivalry propositions is not about merely understanding customer *needs* or *satisfaction* or *dissatisfaction* with the options available in the market. It is about (a) understanding value curves that exist in the minds of different customer segments; (b) along benefit dimensions for benefits available in the market and potential benefits that could be made available, but do not exist as yet; and (c) understanding where on the value curves competitors and the *industry average* operate.

- *Suppliers and customers perceive the resultant benefits from product features differently:* The reason that apparently sure-shot rivalry propositions do not work in the market is the gap between customers' processing of the benefits of an offering and the suppliers' assumptions about them. We had a client who made scooters in collaboration with a Japanese auto major. He said his rivalry proposition over the market leader company was that his technology and vehicles were modern, next-generation, state of the art. He believed that this meant more safety, more convenience and greater riding comfort and manoeuvrability. Consumers, however, interpreted this as having to depend on large auto dealers for even the most minute repairs because the roadside mechanic would not perhaps know how to repair centrally mounted engines, electric start, variator technology, etc. Furthermore, they felt that they were being forced to pay more for *frills* like direction indicators and retractable headlights. The body of the scooter was not made of the familiar sturdy steel, but a polymer, and this again was seen as a problem by the consumers who did not wish to risk damaging their vehicle. Clearly, part of the pain of being a product pioneer is to have to re-programme the benefit processing algorithm that exists in the customer's head.

On the other hand, sometimes companies make the reverse mistake. They do not offer 'advanced' value propositions because they believe consumers are 'not evolved enough' for them. 'No human intervention, it is between you and a machine' is an attractive proposition for lower-income consumers in financial services because they say that men discriminate against poor people with small ticket transactions, but machines do not.

- *Different customers process value from benefits differently:* As we discussed in the case of costs, different customers value the same benefit differently. This statement actually does not need much explanation. It is intuitively obvious and as the old English proverb says, 'One man's meat is another man's poison!' Therefore, the rivalry proposition has to be developed for *a* segment of the market—for a chosen *where to compete* arena (defined in customer-centric terms). Companies tend to forget that rivalry or value propositions are not developed for the business, but for the customer segment that the business chooses to serve.

THE STRUGGLE OF STRATEGY: CRAFTING THE PROFITABLE RIVALRY PROPOSITION

The struggle of strategy is to be able to develop a value proposition, or rather, a rivalry proposition, which is (a) superior to the proposition delivered by competition, (b) sustainable over time and yet (c) profitable for the company.

We have seen the game new entrants play when they enter a market with entrenched incumbents—they offer superior quality at the same price or the same quality at far lower prices, or, if the new entrant has really deep pockets, even superior quality at lower prices. The speed with which market share moves to the new entrant is usually quite amazing, especially if the new entrant is a known, familiar company (for example, ITC entering the biscuits market or Reliance when it entered the telecom market) and the product or service category has no risk-related switching costs that add negative consumer perceived value.

However, sustaining this game is always tough unless the new entrant has some structural or technological advantage that enables them to actually produce at a lower cost. In the absence of this, the losses mount in equal proportion to market success. Companies then tend to respond by decreasing the value offered through a combination

111

of decreasing quality a bit and increasing price a bit, or playing around with variables like grammage per pack. The assumption seems to be that a double-digit market share, built on the back of a clear value advantage, will, in some way, prevent consumers from defecting back to their original choices when the value advantage is reduced. Nothing is further from the truth. A value proposition or rivalry proposition that *buys* market share is not a business-market strategy at all. And yet, it is often justified as a deep-pockets strategy.

Even without playing the 'Let's lose money and build market share' game in a deliberate fashion, the question of balancing customer delight and profitability is a key challenge of developing a winning rivalry proposition, that is at the core of a winning *how to compete* strategy. One of our clients, a finance director in a large company, used to listen to all talk of value propositions and dismiss us as 'bleeding heart consumer liberals!' With good reason too, no doubt. That is why we thought that we must add the qualifier *winning yet profitable* to rivalry propositions. Let us articulate this obvious tension between *winning* and *profitable*, and then explore how to overcome the contradictions.

We know that customers always want the moon for a mere six pence. However, they are also reasonable human beings who understand the rules of the market game, and so they are willing to settle for 'more value than others are offering me'. Thus, they will keep moving to the best value offer that they perceive.

In an evolved market with many competitors of all types, every trick in the book has already been used to try and create the value advantage. The unorganized sector creates value advantage by decreasing benefits and costs

(VA = B"" – C""). The modern discount retailer holds on to most benefits, but decreases costs a lot (VA = B= – C""), hence creating value advantage. The premium player on the other hand does the exact opposite of the discounter (VA = B"" – C""). The regular mainstream players typically tinker around in a narrow band of benefit and cost options (VA = B ± – C±).

So, to create a value advantage, first, one has to choose the generic strategy by which value advantage can be created (Table 5.1) and then create the advantageous value bundle of benefits and costs *within* that framework, that is, make the customer perceive that the (B – C) option is better. This must also be profitable for the company.

Table 5.1: Generic Strategies for Creating Value Advantage	
Type of Company	**Generic Strategy**
Unorganized	VA = B↓↓ – C↓↓
Discounter	VA = B= – C↓↓
Mainstream	VA = B± – C±
High-end Mainstream	VA = B↑ – C↑
Premium	VA = B↑↑ – C↑↑

The task of offering a winning rivalry proposition profitably requires optimizing (or juggling) the following variables:

1. **The benefits–costs package** that the consumer sees as value advantageous, especially the price and the features needed to make the 'cost' perception work (for example, low-priced oil that is thick and viscous is rejected by customers as too costly to use since oil sticks to the sides of the pan, and, therefore, more oil is needed to coat the

same quantity of food; or the low-cost industrial boiler, which is rejected because it takes too much space in the factory).

2. **The cost at which it can be produced** and the cost at which it can be delivered to customers (cost of financing, cost of transportation, cost of distribution, etc.).

Therefore, the key areas of focus when designing winning yet profitable rivalry propositions are:

1. *Choosing benefit and cost dimensions that provide maximum value to the customer and add the least cost to the supplier:* For instance, a free porter service that helps you with heavy baggage even when you fly economy class, and especially when you fly business class, is low

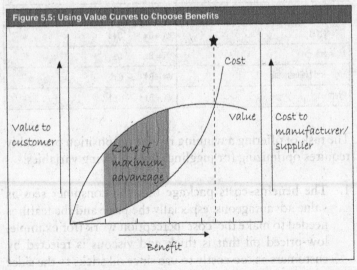

Figure 5.5: Using Value Curves to Choose Benefits

Note: ★ Point beyond which value increases do not make business sense.

114

cost in the Indian context of cheap unskilled labour, and immensely beneficial to the consumer. Or, free Internet in a budget hotel, given how low telecom costs are in India and how e-mail addicted white collar Indians are. Or an e-guru service to help customers learn when they buy a new cell phone, which is a similar low-cost value-adding solution using bright young college kids. A steel supplier might choose to manage steel inventory for a nuts-and-bolts manufacturer, which, again, is cheap in this age of IT-enabled vendor–customer connectivity. An automobile dealer we know provides the coconut, the lemon, the garland of flowers *and* the priest for the new car buyer to do a *puja* to remove the evil eye, even before they leave the showroom. This is indeed intelligent value-adding, and the opposite of value destruction that some of his fellow dealers do when they do not even remove all the traces of dirt from the car after it arrives from a distant godown—a simple enough thing to do, the absence of which creates a disappointment at first sight to the new buyer of the car, who feels like he is spending good money to buy a used car!

In subsequent sections of this chapter, and in later chapters, we will discuss methodologies to sense customer value processing and to identify dimensions on which winning rivalry propositions can be built.

However, before we do that, we want to connect this quest to minimize cost to company and maximize perceived benefit to customers with the discussion on value curves earlier in this chapter. Understanding value curves as they exist in customers' heads and understanding the costs incurred by the supplier in order to deliver incremental benefits are the basis for making choices on what benefits to offer (Figure 5.5).

2. *Working on the insides of the business to strip all possible excess costs in manufacturing, distribution, and customer service relating to the delivering of the benefit:* A leading detergent company decided to add high-quality perfume to their mid-priced detergent bar aimed at lower-middle-class housewives who washed clothes by hand and did not have a washing machine. Adding a 'Keeps clothes smelling delightfully fresh' perfume would give it a customer perceived value advantage over others and give them a platform on which to build this segment of the fabric care business. Perfume, however, adds a lot to the cost of the product even as it adds a lot of value to the customer. The company finally innovated a manufacturing process whereby the perfume could be added in the last stages of manufacturing so as to cut evaporation losses by almost half. However, there are companies that manage to destroy the benefit in the process of cutting costs. Exceptional service is promised at very reasonable prices and hence the winning rivalry proposition is created. Outsourcing of the service is done to decrease the costs of delivering this exceptional service, but very often when it cuts costs, it also starts subtracting customer perceived value. We know of an air-conditioning company that has its high-quality, low-cost winning rivalry proposition. However, in an attempt to offer this proposition profitably, the company has created a low-cost service structure by having the troubleshooting brains, that is, a few highly talented people located in the back office operating the customer-facing front end with service mechanics who are less experienced, lower-cost people who are given cell phones and told to call and describe problems to the central brain cell and get

116

troubleshooting instructions. Perfect in theory, what this does not factor in is the annoyance to customers of having someone standing on a stool in the middle of the living room for hours together talking loudly on a cell phone. This low-cost structure converts a potentially low profit but winning rivalry proposition into an actually higher profit but losing rivalry proposition.

PUTTING IT ALL TOGETHER INTO A PROFITABLE RIVALRY PROPOSITION: SOME EXAMPLES

A leading biscuit company has defined its *how to compete* proposition, valid across the board for all customer or consumption segments (including the *sheer indulgence* segment) as *the healthier, tastier snacking option*. The 'B' (benefit to customers) is clear. The 'C' (cost to customers) is that price points will be matched, but a lower customer perceived cost will be achieved by designing all packaging will be done in such a way that wastage in use is minimized (for instance, a big pack with five servings of three biscuits each in a mini pack made of tin foil).

An IT major in India, in the software outsourcing business, describes its value proposition to its overseas customers as executing projects with total predictability (no unpleasant surprises because of deviations from the time and cost plan as the project progresses), offering de-risked solutions (no possibility that after the full solution has been developed, it runs the risk of not working well because of some unforeseen context in which it has to operate), scalable solutions (can build on these solutions as the needs grow, rather than having to abandon it and build a new solution)—all this at a far lower cost than what the local IT vendors operating in that market are charging. While this rivalry proposition works against competitors who are American and European software developers with much higher cost structures, it does not provide a customer perceived value advantage over the big Indian competitors, all of whom offer these benefits in varying degrees at the same cost, and even smaller Indian competitors who offer about 60 per cent of the benefit at 40 per cent of the cost. The problem to solve for would be 'how to create a value advantage over local competitors, both big and small—what dimensions of B and what dimensions of C to offer at what levels in order to achieve that without sacrificing the margins?' Part of the solution lies in segmenting the market and not participating in those projects where benefit sensitivity is low on the part of customers, and winning more of those projects that are mission critical, and, hence, more benefit sensitive than price sensitive. Part of the solution lies in re-programming the customer and changing his value-processing algorithm through different kinds of pricing, including pricing per transaction that the software does (that is, earning revenue during the use of the software and pricing lower at the time of building it), etc. Part of the solution lies in actually deciding which combination of benefits to offer at a higher level than others and yet maintain profitability based on the 'cost to us—value to the customer' assessment that we have talked about earlier. The IT company, however, phrases this as a 'brand differentiation' problem, which it is, but the solution does not lie in better talk (communication to the customer); it lies in creating the more valuable walk (better B–C proposition that is still profitable).

For most B2B companies, the generic rivalry proposition is that *we help you earn more money than you will if you do not use us (and use one of our competitors)*. The challenge here is the value package or the combination of 'B' and 'C' elements that needs to be strung together to achieve this. Another generic proposition for B2B, and typically a *vendor* proposition is, 'We help you sleep better because we take care of all your worries.' Again, how this generic rivalry proposition is *actually delivered* in a value package that is both superior and profitable is the question. It, therefore, helps to think more sharply about what a less generic, more differentiated proposition could be in order to enable commanding higher prices, and still retaining the value advantage.

In the case of a polyurethane supplier who supplies the raw material to footwear exporters, the generic proposition of 'Buy from us, we help you make more money' could easily be operationalized not in the territory of decreasing C, but in the territory of improving B. Consumer insight shows that one of the reasons that business profitability is low for footwear exporters is that they do not have the know-how to execute some of the export order they bag. This makes it an expensive process of trial and error, with instances of consignments being rejected by the buyers. Therefore, the generic proposition translates as 'We help you fulfil even the most technically difficult order', coming from a key raw material supplier, is both a winning proposition and a potentially profitable one. Since usually customers want to go up the value chain on the kind of orders they get, they are willing to pay a price premium for the suppliers who can help them do so. Often, the smart supplier who understands how customers process cost and who understands his own cost structure will re-position the price premium in terms of shorter credit periods or three-year fixed price lock-in contracts or even result-based fees, that is, helping in decreasing rejections and benefits accruing to be shared equally.

Nirma's rivalry proposition is 'adequate quality at affordable prices'. As a consumer once said: There is no way of figuring out or measuring that a bed sheet washed in Nirma will last less than the one washed with Surf, since bed sheets last for years and years anyway! This is clearly a case of understanding how consumers process value rather than how suppliers think they *ought* to be processing value.

WILL EDUCATING CUSTOMERS IMPROVE THEIR APPRECIATION THE VALUE PROPOSITION?

A lot of businesses, particularly MNC businesses entering India nowadays, on finding that the facts of value delivered by their proposition are not perceived in the same way by customers, believe that customer education is the answer. Often what they term as 'value ignorance' is also what we term 'value arrogance', that is, not understanding the sophistication with which Indian consumers process value and not recognizing the real value provided by apparently backward local players, whether it is the small *kirana* store or the man who services your laptop sitting in your home. However, to link the task of educating the consumer, in terms of what we have been discussing, education is about re-programming customers' hard disks and getting them to process value differently to arrive at a different answer. Sometimes, when there has been a misreading of the offer or its features, this might be easily done. But very often, changing the value processing algorithm embedded in the consumers' heads is very hard. This algorithm has been developed over years based on the user's own experience. Understanding those foundations is critical to finding ways to change it. It is the supplier who needs to be educated in many cases and not the consumers! In cases where the consumer is genuinely misinformed or unaware, education can work and will do the job very quickly.

120

CHAPTER 6

Designing the Value Package and Value Delivery System

In the previous chapters, we have talked about how the business-market strategy is the 'front end' of a business strategy, akin to the engine of a train that pulls the rest of the train in a particular direction; the different compartments of the train that follow the path set by the business-market strategy engine are the functional area strategies. With this analogy, it is easy to understand what the frequently used term 'aligning the organization with the strategy' actually means. With our view of strategy, it means that every function in the organization should be designed such that it is able to support the delivering of the business-market strategy. In earlier chapters we have referred to this as Value Delivery System (VDS).

RECAP: The business-market strategy is the way a business as a whole or an SBU chooses to compete in the market, or, to use analogy, it is the choice of playgrounds and games that it chooses to play in the market. We discussed two key elements or decisions to be made when designing the business-market strategy, that is, the choices of where in

Figure 6.1: The CBBS Framework: Value Delivery System

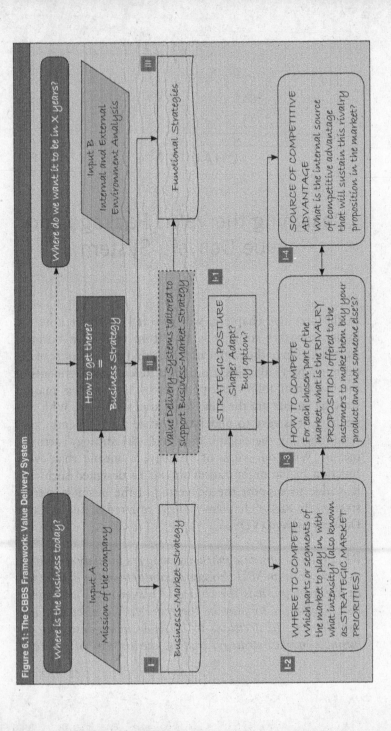

Where is the business today?

Where do we want it to be in X years?

Input A
Mission of the company

Input B
Internal and External Environment Analysis

I
How to get there?
=
Business Strategy

II
Value Delivery Systems tailored to support Business-Market Strategy

III
Functional Strategies

I
Business-Market Strategy

I-1
STRATEGIC POSTURE
Shape? Adapt?
Buy option?

I-2
WHERE TO COMPETE
Which parts or segments of the market to play in, with what intensity? (also known as STRATEGIC MARKET PRIORITIES)

I-3
HOW TO COMPETE
For each chosen part of the market, what is the RIVALRY PROPOSITION offered to the customers to make them buy your product and not someone else's?

I-4
SOURCE OF COMPETITIVE ADVANTAGE
What is the internal source of competitive advantage that will sustain this rivalry proposition in the market?

the market/customer universe/needs universe to compete, with what intensity; and in each chosen part of the market, crafting how to compete by designing rivalry propositions that pro- vide customer perceived value advantage over competition.

Now it is time to take this a step further and design how to walk the talk of all the promises to the customer. Since customers do not buy strategy documents but buy products and services, the next step of business-market strategy is to translate the rivalry proposition and the $V = B - C$ equations on which it is based into products and services with specific features and resultant benefits and with a set of costs, which include not just the price, but all other costs of usage. We call this the *value package*.

The value package is just another phrase for product and service bundles, but it reminds us that we must see products and services the way our customers see them—*as a bundle of benefits and costs*. This is what is often referred to as 'product strategy' in many companies.

However, we notice that all too often, product strategy is not as rigorously linked to business-market strategy as it should be. It is linked with competitor offerings and how to better them or with which product segments of the market offer highest margins (or growth).

Once the value packages to be offered are designed, the next step is to design every part of the organization's internal operations and customer facing operations to be able to help deliver and communicate the value proposition to each of the chosen parts of the market. We have discussed earlier how a customer-centric business must view itself as a value delivery system (VDS), where every part of it is designed and tuned in order to deliver the chosen value or rivalry proposition to consumers. Therefore, a 'fun dining' restaurant business must have recruitment processes to be able to recruit staff who are socially confident and have a sense of humour; and a low-margin high-volume business must have finance people who understand how to manage a business where net margins will be negative until serious scale has been built but yet understand financial risk in such businesses.

This chapter discusses both the value package development and the design of VDS in greater detail, building on the discussion in Chapter 3. We do believe, though, that a far better place to read about this in depth is in the book *Delivering Profitable Value: A Revolutionary Framework to Accelerate Growth, Generate Wealth and Rediscover the Heart of Business* by Michael J. Lanning (2000).

DESIGNING THE VALUE PACKAGE

Since most situations relate to ongoing businesses and not to greenfield businesses, the first step to concretizing the rivalry proposition of the business is to evaluate the current portfolio of offerings to the customer and see if they are faithful to the proposition. In many cases, there is a huge slip between the cup and the lip. We worked with a large and successful company that was competing in the talent market. Its winning rivalry proposition was:

A job with us offers a unique combination of opportunities to build new knowledge and opportunities to leverage it for business growth. (We will use the short hand of K + B for this proposition, in the rest of this discussion.) We enable you to build knowledge and we empower you to leverage it for business growth. Therefore, a job with us will develop in you this unique combination of skills and make you even more valuable in the job market, should you choose to leave.

The first step to translating this to reality was to check if this K + B package was actually present in jobs currently offered by the company. Here is how not to do it. The company hired a consulting firm and, to begin with, asked them to analyse all the marketing jobs, since that was where their star talent would reside. They did a classical job content analysis asking the question 'what are all the components of this job', and provided a pie chart of how much time was spent on creating advertising, designing brand promotions, coordination with sales, etc., and suggested some improvements in the mix. However, if they had thought of the business as a VDS, and had they been more customer-centric, they would have analysed all the jobs in terms of their ability to deliver the K + B proposition—building knowledge (K component) and leveraging it for business growth (B component). Had they also been more customer-centric, they would have first understood what dimensions the customers themselves used to analyse their jobs and built solutions around those. When done that way, it was clear that most marketing roles did not deliver the proposition to the talent market customer (potential employee) at all. When asked how *they* analysed their jobs, employees came up with four buckets of work that they did. First was what they called 'cerebral ops' where they said 60 per cent of their time went in complex logistical thinking and coordination between different parts of the company to keep the business engine running. While this was critical grease that needed to be applied to the wheels of business operations, it required the high operational intelligence that a super administrative assistant would have and the MBA doing that job currently was over-qualified for it. While there was some K + B component to it in terms of designing processes that would make all this work better, the bulk of it failed to deliver the proposition. The next bucket of their work, another 30 per cent of it, was making PowerPoint slides for their bosses to use at *their* meetings to which the brand managers were not invited. While there was certainly an intellectual content to it, there was not either much K or much B in it. Another 10 per cent of their work was working on special initiatives that the company was undertaking and tasks relating to it being cascaded all the way down the organization. Examples of these were integration of processes of companies that had been acquired, or HR projects like improving creativity and innovation and so on. While potentially these had great K and B components, in reality they did not deliver because of the way they were administered. The CPU or brains of the initiative resided in only one place, with one senior manager and his team sitting abroad at global HQ, and everyone else was viewed as implementation arms and legs.

The task, therefore, was to map all the outputs expected from each job, and build the K + B component into each element of it. Therefore, the special projects could be more decentralized and the assembling of the whole piece be made more transparent and more participative; the 'cerebral ops' which consumed 60 per cent of time could be transferred to a special cadre of super administrators for whom the K + B would lie in bringing continuous improvements in process as well; and new components be built into each job to truly make it the 'create new knowledge and leverage for business growth' K + B value package. For example, whenever competitors launched a new product in any market, young area sales managers said they designed a 'welcome package' for it! This is an area with a serious 'how to' K component, and a serious B component 'Consumer insight' is another valuable bucket that has a K + B component built into it that could be embedded into the job description.

To take another example, a company which says its rivalry proposition is 'superior reliability and functionality' will need to translate this into a package of a set of concrete benefits and guarantees and a price and use cost that consumers will perceive to be superior functionality and reliability (and of course deliver it at a cost which is profitable for the company). In order to get the value package right, companies need to know what consumers think about when they think about functionality and reliability. They also need to be innovative and find new ways of delivering these, and they need to also check with customers that they agree with what the company thinks is better—functionality or reliability.

'Easy to use and comes with a phone number you can call and someone will guide you through whatever you want to do' could be a better way to deliver superior functionality, as the consumer sees and interprets functionality, rather than through the addition of new features. Therefore, recruiting smart and articulate young people at the other end of the helpline, and training them well, would be a key part of the VDS.

We know of a hotel that thinks it delivers superior functionality by having a single electronic console for everything in the room, including the lights. However, a person groggy in the middle of the night, wanting to quickly check the time, needs to navigate through a bunch of drop-down menus just so he can switch the light on and needs his brains switched on before the light is switched on. That is not superior functionality to a whole bunch of people, for sure! When hotels say that they are a 'home away from home' and that is their rivalry proposition, they need to understand whether the value package should contain a menu with lots of varieties of simple food or whether it should have food served within five minutes of placing the order.

MAPPING 'RESULTANT EXPERIENCES'

Here is another way to think through designing a value package, which we have found very helpful:

In his book *Delivering Profitable Value* (2000), Michael J. Lanning describes the rivalry proposition or the value proposition as comprising a set of 'resultant consumer experiences' that the company then needs to figure out how it will deliver through what set of internal actions. Hence, a hospital with a rivalry proposition of 'we do everything possible to make you feel better' could have a set of resultant experiences like 'feel reassured that you are getting exactly the right treatment', 'have no anxiety about logistics for yourself or the care givers in your family', and 'pay in instalments if you are a card holder of Company X'.

We suggest that even if the first cut of arriving at a rivalry proposition is a 'catchall', generic construct such as 'superior reliability', the competitive advantage could still come from how it is translated into a set of resulting customer experiences. This way of thinking provides far richer differentiation than the competition and also enables out-of-the-box thinking. So 'superior reliability', in the context of laptops, could be expressed as a resulting customer experience of 'never be in a situation where you have something important stuck in your laptop that you cannot retrieve urgently'. This then could lead to a value package design, which includes a special memory that is an automatic backup of recent contents or important items that can be hooked up to another computer easily; or a special plug through which other power cords can be used in an emergency if the battery runs out and the cord is not available. Superior reliability could also be a resulting customer experience as a result of immediate service or support within two hours, and a replacement laptop of the same model until the contents on the hard disk are extracted. It could also be a resultant customer experience of a 'use with abandon' delivered through an extra-robust frame and case.

These are just some examples to illustrate a way of thinking through the translation of a value proposition into a value package. In his book, Lanning discusses the resultant customer experiences of South West Airline as: (a) save travel time (door-to-door); (b) be amused; (c) as safe as the safest airline; (d) less comfort than any other airline; and (e) price approximately the same as the cost of driving, about 30 per cent lower than other airlines. The critical next question is how can each of these be delivered? This is the VDS of an organization. Lanning points out that the difference between market winners and losers is often not the uniqueness of their value proposition, but how good their VDS is in delivering resultant customer experiences, that is, their ability to walk their talk. He says:

> [O]ne can hoist a value proposition like a flag and insist that everyone salute it, but that will not change much

an organization's chances of success. Rather, to go beyond the lip service and genuinely deliver a chosen value proposition, all aspects and elements of the business [products, services, processes, resources] must be specifically designed to provide and communicate the proposition to customers. (Lanning 2000: 88)

DESIGNING THE VALUE DELIVERY SYSTEM

As we discussed in Chapter 3 where we introduced the idea of VDS, the CBBS view of organizations is that they are VDSs and not a bunch of functional silos (see Figure 6.1).

The functional silos view of the organization supposes that each silo must do all it can to maximize its own efficiency and operate using its own metrics; while the VDS view of organization supposes that the best metric of effectiveness of a function is its ability to help the organization deliver the chosen and promised value to the customer.

Therefore, if one of the resultant experiences of a value proposition of a paint company is 'get exactly the shade you imagined in your head', then the finance folk cannot reduce working capital in the system by reducing the inventory of slow-moving items. Different parts of the organization will have to work together for a base paint and tinting machine system to be established at each point of sale—with all the resultant requirements for capex, for persuading dealers to invest in the capex, for training them, for convincing customers to visit shops, for painters to move away from shade cards, etc. Simple as this may sound, it actually requires a huge paradigm shift in the organization at many levels.

Instead of a paint company, imagine a watch or a jewellery company whose rivalry proposition is unmatched variety and novelty. Actually, we do know of one such company who then had the big consulting firm come in to do an operational performance improvement programme with a fee, which was a percentage of the working capital released. They did an A–B–C analysis of the designs and then decided to drop several of them since they predictably found that 65 per cent of the sales came from 20 per cent of the items.

However, had they held a VDS view of the world, they would have understood perhaps the value, in the case of the jewellery business, of potential for margin increases through fixed prices to the consumer and smart buying of gold using

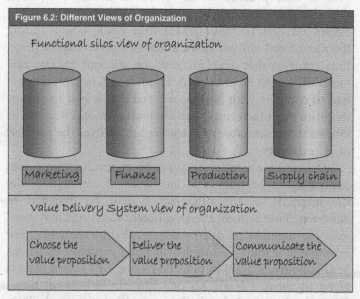

Figure 6.2: Different Views of Organization

Functional silos view of organization

Marketing | Finance | Production | Supply chain

Value Delivery System view of organization

Choose the value proposition → Deliver the value proposition → Communicate the value proposition

Source: Adapted from Lanning (2000).

sophisticated financial instruments; or in the case of watches, the marketing and the design folks would have sat together and figured out how to make the least amount of changes or the least costly changes but still achieve a customer perception of newness. Of course what compounded this problem further was the design- and model-led advertising that the company did. Customers walked into the shop with copies of the ads and pointed to specific models that they wanted which, when unavailable, led to lost sales and lost credibility for the brand.

The value proposition of Nirma was 'affordable price, adequate quality' and the promise was to deliver detergent powder at one-third the price of the market leader. Nirma actually had a different distribution model compared to the FMCG 'best practice/model'. It relied on dumping large quantities at a central point in the wholesale market and asking retailers to come and collect stock, compensating them at a fixed rate per kilo and not as a percentage of price, thus ensuring that price increases on account of, say, raw material, would be contained. Hindustan Unilever, when it had to compete with Nirma, realized that it had to change its entire manufacturing to an outsourced model because its internal costs structure was too high to deliver the promise of affordability.

Delivering the value requires every resultant customer experience to be translated into a set of actions on *how* the internals of the organization will be designed to deliver it. Five actions in five different functions may need to come together to deliver one resultant experience. For example, a leading IT supplier in India promises its clients predictability, scalability and de-risking of IT assignments given to them. Clearly no one silo can deliver all these. Similarly, Lanning's book shows, in his analysis of SWA, how the resultant experience of 'saves time' was achieved through a combination of (a) having an entire fleet of the same type of aircraft so that turnaround time between flights was minimized; (b) using small airports in the city so that door-to-door time for passengers could be minimized; and (c) not issuing boarding passes and pre-assigned seats. As can be seen from this list, it cuts across different silos of a traditional organization.

COMMUNICATING THE VALUE

The view of a business as a VDS has three parts to it, as we have discussed in Chapter 2 (see Figure 6.3).

The first part of the figure flows from the *how to compete* decision on what is the value proposition or the rivalry proposition that the business promises its customers.

The second part of the VDS deals with the translation of the promised value proposition into the value package, that is, the actual product features and costs, and the designing of the VDS that will actually deliver the proposition to the consumer. The third part is to communicate this rivalry proposition to customers. As people in today's world of businesses are increasingly beginning to appreciate, communicating what an organization's rivalry proposition is, is about a lot more than advertising. In fact, it may not even be about advertising. It is, in services businesses, about the signalling that gets done at every point of the business-customer interface. A hospitals business that says it is good value for money and understands how expensive medical care is to the normal person, had better cease and desist from having large expanses of marble or granite in its lobby area, even if those are the easiest to keep clean. A health care business that says 'because we are more trustworthy than others' had better hire and train a bunch of medical communicators who will patiently explain all procedures and why they need to be done to patients and their families. *B2B businesses have to communicate their value through every single interface point, mostly sales people and staff. They need to be trained to act as live signallers of the company's proposition.*

An IT company we know, which wanted to fight its rivals with the rivalry proposition that 'we help you to transform your business through IT', communicated this by sponsoring a business transformation award in partnership with an Ivy League business school, and a star-studded jury of CEOs of companies who had successfully transformed their own businesses. A B2B company that says its rivalry proposition is that its customers are delighted with them, must be able to showcase, in several ways, its customers for potential customers to see. Titan watches decided to deliver its value proposition of 'an anywhere in the world watch company that just happens to be in India' through resultant experiences of a wide range of 'never seen before'

Figure 6.3: The Value Delivery System View of Business

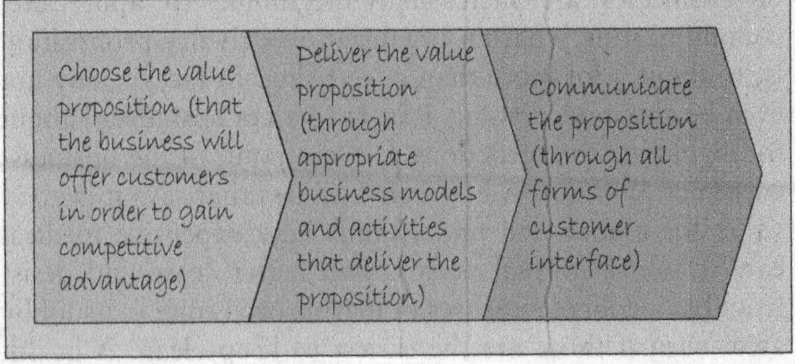

Choose the value proposition (that the business will offer customers in order to gain competitive advantage) / Deliver the value proposition (through appropriate business models and activities that deliver the proposition) / Communicate the proposition (through all forms of customer interface)

Source: Adapted from Lanning (2000).

designs, and it chose its retail outlets as the primary means of communicating the value. As their then MD said, you have to take the shop to the customer to get the customer to the shop. So advertising was limited to advertising retail outlet counters and ambience.

POSTSCRIPT

Clearly this approach of running of a business as a value delivery system requires real commitment to the chosen strategy and at the heart of strategy is sacrifice. It means walking down a particular path because that will eventually be what will get you to the destination in the best shape, even if for any given part of the way there is some other path that looks more picturesque or better paved. Indian businesses are notoriously unwilling to stick to a path. They always say: 'Yes, yes, this is the main thing, I agree. But what is the harm in *also* doing a bit of that as well?' It ends up usually like the sign in a restaurant we drove past recently: 'Pisces Seafood Restaurant [appetizing picture of a tandoori fish]—specialists in vegetarian food also.'

CHAPTER 7

The Science and Art of Strategic Business-Market Segmentation

The *where to compete* decision, as was discussed in Chapter 4, is a key element of business-market strategy and it defines which parts of the market or the playgrounds the company will play in, and prioritizes them. Central to the *where to compete* decision is a process of customer-based business-market segmentation that we have discussed conceptually, in great detail, in Chapter 4.

To recap, it involves carving the usually heterogeneous market into more homogeneous sub-markets in a way that helps companies to design targeted and focussed consumer offerings, and, hence, drive growth, improve profitability, and create long-term competitive advantage. This done, the company then has to decide: (a) which of these sub-markets it wants to compete in and which it wants to stay out of; (b) with what relative intensity to compete in each of the chosen sub-markets; and (c) how to compete in each chosen sub-market so as to create customer perceived value advantage over competition (discussed in Chapter 5). The end result of good business-market segmentation is to create

Figure 7.1: The CBBS Framework: Business-Market Segmentation

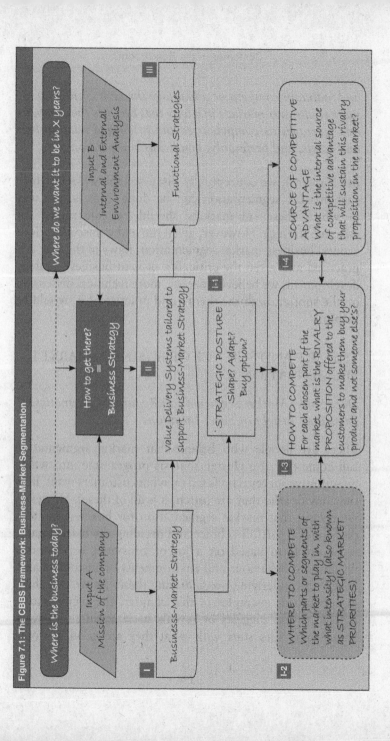

and maintain competitive advantage through cutting up the market into sub-markets in a way that benefits the company and leverages its competencies and privileged relationships and assets; and preferably, handicaps competition too.

In Chapter 4, we conceptually discussed the ways in which such market segmentation can be done, that is, the way in which these sub-markets should be constructed for effective strategy. However, given the many misconceptions around business-market segmentation, flaws in the way it is practised and given the criticality of it to business strategy development, we believe a deeper, more technical discussion on the subject, both the theory and practice of it, would be helpful.

THE ART AND SCIENCE OF BUSINESS-MARKET SEGMENTATION

Does Smart Market Segmentation Require Mathematics, Consumer Insight or Sheer Intuition?

There are people who believe that market segmentation can come out of a cluster analysis programme into which quantitative survey data is fed on what customers want, how they buy or who they are (often, it is all of these). However, we believe that market segmentation for business strategy decisions of portfolio choice and deciding the market game is an art form based on a lot of consumer or customer insight into behaviour and environments of customers and, hence, the underlying needs driving these. As we will show in subsequent examples in this chapter, the segmentation scheme to use suggests or reveals itself in different ways. Some companies start with what they are good at doing and then reach out to customers who will value these products. Some start with observing the different varieties of consumer purchase behaviour that exist and then drill down to what the fundamental needs are that drive these different behaviours, and, hence, construct need segments. In B2B businesses, we find that starting with different end users and studying what kind of business *they* run (which customers they serve, how they compete to win) leads to sensible segmentation schemes. In yet other cases, asking consumers why they use a category and what they use as a basis for brand choice leads to defining a segmentation scheme.

On methodology, our advice is to stay away from using formulaic, cookie-cutter approaches which say, for example, that there are five ways to segment the market: segment consumers based on the key buying factors they use when deciding or segment based on a grid of *geography × end use industry × size of customer*, etc. This should be quite obvious if we think about the end game or the deliverables of good market segmentation— that it needs to be customized for what your company is good at doing and needs to be a scheme that is not in your competitors' interest to adopt. We also advise against diving straightaway into mathematical multivariate models. What we are trying to achieve here is to construct a *mental model* of the market first. Once such segmentation is developed based on customer insight—which is an art form too in many ways—then quantitative methods can be used to validate their existence and determine their size and profile. We are not saying that customer insight must be developed only using qualitative methodologies. Consumer insight can be based on hard quantitative analysis of customer behaviour, shop observations, ethnographic studies, the strategist's gut instincts or the manager's experiences on what drives customer choices, cultural analysis, historical performance of different types of products, and so on. Typically, it is a combination of all these factors. We are merely saying that arriving at market segmentation schemes, like any other element of the strategy development process, cannot come out of a plug-and-play quantitative model or survey. As we have discussed in Chapter 4, market segments are not something that are inherently the property of the market (that is to say, not something that is intrinsic to a market). Segmentation is a verb. That is to say one has to 'do segmentation' of the market. Imagine cutting up a giant chocolate cake to serve at a party with lots of guests— different people will cut it in different ways, using different implements and different methods. The resultant pieces will differ from each other as well *and* be different depending on who cut it up using what logic.

Companies must, therefore, segment the market in such a way that they get competitive advantage through the segmentation scheme they choose.

There are, however, certain conceptual ideas about market segmentation that must be used as pole stars to navigate through the journey of market segmentation. In the rest of the chapter, we will first examine concepts to guide the segmentation journey and then provide examples of these journeys to further illustrate the concepts.

Concept 1: Discovering Avenues of Discontinuous Growth by Defining the Market Universe Using Customer Variables, Preferably Customer Perceived 'Need Spaces'

The way the market universe is defined is key to a competitively advantageous *where to compete* decision. If the universe is defined narrowly, and using product variables, for example, 'buyers or intending buyers of Product X', then it will be very hard to find 'beyond the usual', what nobody else in the industry has seen segments like, for example, high-value segments or segments where it is possible to easily create significant competitive advantage or segments which offer potential for discontinuous growth. Hence this discussion on how to define the market universe—before deciding how to segment.

Markets are not made up of products or price points or competitor sets or geographies or technologies—they are made up of people who have needs that they are trying to fulfil. We will, therefore, refer to market universes henceforth as *need space* or *need arenas* or *value spaces*. However, all too often, for the purposes of developing business strategy, companies usually tend to define their market universe not as 'people having need X', but as 'people buying Product X or using Technology Y or buying from Competitor X'. We find this definition very limiting and myopic because it ignores avenues for growth via market expansion by creating special offers for people who have the need, but not the ability or desire to buy what is on offer by the suppliers.

For example, by defining its market universe using traditional industry-defined boundaries of the market as 'current and potential plane travellers,' would SWA have found the market segment which formed the cornerstone of its highly differentiated business strategy i.e., car travellers who lay outside the boundary of the traditionally defined market?

By thinking of the potential market as 'all people' (whether they travel by air or want to or never want to) and studying their travel habits, they managed to identify or discover a segment of non-air travellers that they could dominate and grow from. These were the frequent travellers who drove by car between two cities not very far apart, and point to point, and were mostly business travellers. We must hasten to add that the genius of SWA was of course not just in uncovering the existence of this segment, but even more so in creating an airline business model that could deliver a consumer-perceived value advantage over the car—quicker travel, more convenient, same cost and more fun.

To take another example, and this time, one that got it wrong: Tractor companies in India call themselves sellers of farm equipment and services and farm solutions, etc., yet they invariably define their market universe as potential buyers of tractors. Were they to define their market universe as farmers with a need to reduce physical effort as well as to improve yield and, hence financial returns, they would build into their business strategy the fact that the overwhelming majority of Indian farmers have very small landholdings on which tractors do not work or are uneconomical; who have no mechanization, and who have a very strong need not to do arduous physical labour or not use bullocks, and to somehow join the march of modernity happening all around them. This creates a market which needs to be catered to with a 'Below the Tractor Line' business of perhaps power tillers or threshers and sprayers, and so on, perhaps using a rental business model. If done successfully, this could result in quantum growth for a true farm equipment and services and solutions company. Further, this makes tractor companies *own a larger base* of customers that they can leverage for new businesses, perhaps that of rural retailing or financial services.

Especially in the case of growth seeking strategies, the definition of market universe should go well beyond current users of the product category or industry-defined product-

142

based boundaries. It should include all people who have needs (problems or desires) and are currently spending money to fulfil them; and should also include those that are not spending money to fulfil them, but have the economic potential to do so.

For example, the market universe for the home air-conditioning business should comprise all people above a certain income group, who live in hot climates, dislike the heat and have the need to do something about it. Some of them who own (that is, have spent money on) cooling gadgets other than air conditioners, or plan to own such gadgets (air coolers for example), should be an obvious part of the market universe. Such people would usually be left out in the standard market universe definition that air-conditioner companies operate with, which is 'intending buyers of air conditioners'. They then bemoan the small and slow-growing market, decide that this business's 'time' has not yet come and they miss out on the huge opportunity of both heat and consumer incomes rising in a large country like India.

The market universe should also include those who do not possess any such implements, but do feel the heat and try various other homegrown ways to keep cool. One very high-value segment of those who have never bought or thought of buying an air conditioner that would emerge from broadening the market universe definition could be that of people who have air-conditioned cars, but not air-conditioned homes (a significant number in India, as even entry-level cars now come factory-fitted with air conditioners).

Another such opportunity segment that would not emerge with narrowly product-based definitions of the market universe would be people who live in coastal areas of the country where the cheaper alternative of air coolers do not work because of the humidity and where even a partial level of cooling (a half-ton air conditioner), as compared to the ideal requirement of a one-ton air conditioner) brings an acceptable level of cooling and level of comfort.

Concept 2: Achieving Competitive Advantage by Segmenting the Market Universe Using Customer Variables Relevant to the Strengths of the Business

Having defined the market universe in terms of customer variables like their needs or their behaviour, preferences, attitudes, etc., the next step is to segment this universe—or cut it up into sub-markets—such that it helps a company maximize the value it can extract from the market, by being able to offer tailor-made offers to suit the needs and requirements of each segment, and to do so in a way that is not easy for competition to copy.

However, we often find, with both our MBA students as well as practicing managers, that they get so engrossed and embroiled in the actual task of performing/deriving/doing market segmentation that they lose sight of the reason why they set out to segment the market in the first place. The net result is that they end up with endless divisions and sub-divisions of the market using every available variable, many of them not necessarily relevant to their business, for example, produce segments or sub-markets based on a plethora of variables like Income X, Age X type of product bought X, First-time user–Re-buyer X, Town-class X application . . . ., and end up confusing themselves thoroughly. This usually happens when the question asked is: 'And in how many different ways can we cut this market? And are there any other knives or blades we can use to cut this further?' And, of course, there always are!

There are two rules here that we are trying to highlight:

1. One, as we have said all through this chapter and Chapter 4—that market segmentation for the purposes of business strategy must have the power to offer avenues of strategic value creation for the company.

2. The second and more technical rule is that market segmentation must yield sub-markets such that consumers *within* each submarket have very similar needs; but *across* sub-markets, consumer needs are starkly different from each other. Further, the people *within* each sub-market should not only want similar things, but also process value using similar algorithms; however, they need not necessarily behave in the same way and use the same things to fulfil their needs. Similarly, people *across* sub-markets should want different things and process value differently. Mathematically put, segmentation makes sense only if intra-segment variance is minimized and inter-segment variance is maximized.

   If intra-segment, that is, intra-sub-market variance is high, then it is merely that the market has been merely cut up into random chunks (no matter how scientifically!) and not into market segments of strategic value, that is, those that help drive growth and/or improve profitability and/or create competitive advantage. If the inter-segment variance is not high, then we do not really not have two market segments at all—and the reason why we broke up the market into sub-markets to begin with, is not accomplished.

However, even if these rules of segmentation are fulfilled, if there is no strategic value creation opportunity as a result of segmentation, it will add more to the cost and complexity of a business than the returns in terms of business value.

Since we describe this process of market segmentation both as a science as well as art, we will take the liberty of now using mental pictures that can intuitively explain what this process is all about.

Mental Picture 1: Cakes and Knives Used to Cut Them!

The market universe is a cake that has to be segmented or cut up (in such a way as to improve competitive advantage) using a knife or a combination of knives that are created from customer variables. For example, the knives used to cut up the market for water-treatment units used in manufacturing plants can either be created from product variables like the type of treatment unit (resin based, reverse osmosis, etc.), customized versus standard units, and so on; or they can—and indeed must—be created from customer variables such as: (a) the nature and complexity of the manufacturing process of the customer, defined along those parameters which determine his needs for water treatment; (b) a variable relating to the ability to spend or affordability of the customer company like, for example, turnover and profitability of the customer company (or the manufacturing unit). Often B2B companies use customer–company turnover and profitability rather blindly as a basis on which to segment their customer market universe. They need to stop and think whether these variables are actually a good proxy for ability to spend or affordability. It is not always obvious that they are. To take a very simple example, a small-sized, moderately profitable company may

146

have a greater propensity to spend on advertising or on upgrading the packaging that it uses, rather than a large, very profitable one; or a large company that is an MNC with fixed international vendors decided by headquarters may not have the freedom to make its own supplier choices, unlike a smaller local domestic company.

How these knives are used, in what combination and sequence, is a matter of the skill and comfort level of the strategist. The only point we would like to emphasize here is that the knives that are used to cut up the market must be created from customer variables, and customized to the situation of the company for which strategy is being developed. We further insist that only those customer variables that are relevant to, and influence the requirements and behaviour of customers with respect to how they purchase be selected. Using customer variables without applying much thought to which ones influence customer attitude and behaviour with respect to the business in question, is not very useful. One might even say that it is of far less use than product variables.

We often find that B2B businesses do tend to segment their market based on standard customer variables like turnover of the customer company and the industry vertical (for example, a telecom or IT services company serving institutional customers could segment its market into five verticals based on end-user industry and big, medium, or small turnover companies within each). This is certainly better than no segmenting at all. It recognizes that the customers in Vertical 1 have different needs and value processing methods than those in Vertical 2, etc. However, market segmentation that stops at just this is merely akin to a doctor saying the market for insulin treatment is the diabetic and the market for sleeping tablets is the person who needs to sleep some more. It is what we call *table stakes* segmentation: it merely qualifies you to enter into the game, but not to win it. It is, however, obviously better than no segmentation at all, but must be viewed as the first step in business-market segmentation.

Mental Picture 2: Oases and Islands!

Business-market segmentation is about extracting islands of exceptionally high value from within the served-market and is fairly homogeneous, usually.

This mental picture of the process of segmentation is about finding oases in the desert—it enables you to think of people and situations that create special needs. The market for processed, ready-to-eat packaged food is homogeneous in its characteristic that housewives in both rich as well as poor homes do not want it for a variety of reasons, and certainly not at the prices at which it is currently being offered. However, due to the phenomenon of centralized entrance exams for engineering and medical colleges in various parts of the country, several hundred thousand students each year are relocated for a five-year period to places far away from home and into parts of India with totally different food habits. North Indian wheat-eating children are assigned to colleges in rice-eating south India, and vice versa, and all of them desperately search for a taste of familiar food. They are a great oasis of value given their large numbers, their concentration in twenty or thirty known college campus towns and the fact that their happiness requires only a limited range of *comfort food* staples. The current price of these ready-to-eat packets is cheaper than the same food served in a restaurant, and is, therefore, of value to these students; their availability at any time of the night or day is seen to be good value for money timings that students keep is also something that matters.

At the Ahmedabad airport, the owner of a small tea stall charges Rs 5 for tea with sugar and Rs 10 for tea *without* sugar. He has figured out that there is a sub-market or a customer segment comprising people who are diabetic or weight-watching, who will do anything to avoid the sugar, and most airports have automatic vending machines where *no sugar* is not an option. It is a very valuable sub-market because tea without sugar costs less to make and also commands a price premium!

In a consulting business or even a financial services business, it is quite well known empirically that the very sophisticated and the very unsophisticated customers are not willing to pay higher prices—they will negotiate down to the last rupee. The *somewhat sophisticated* customers are always the best ones to have. The very sophisticated consumers think they have the same knowledge as the consultant or financial planner, and are not willing to pay more for a slim knowledge advantage that the supplier may have. The very unsophisticated are unable to appreciate or value the knowledge that the consultant or financial planner brings. The middle level of sophistication, therefore, is where the sweet spot of the market lies.

In commoditized chemicals like caustic soda, a sub-market of exceptional value lies in identifying customers who do not want a certain level of purity or those who do not track commodity prices on a daily basis (either because it is a small part of their total cost or because their buying behaviour is long-term price-fixed contracts).

B2B businesses will actually find that their market universe harbours far greater islands of high value—like, for example, small export-oriented units that have to be compliant with international norms and, hence, mimic behaviour that was hitherto the preserve of larger companies: or, for example, customers for whom a particular raw material that they buy from is so small and incidental to their manufacturing process, that they are relatively less price conscious about it, or customers for whom it is the other way around—the raw material or service that they buy from you is so mission-critical and yet is a small part of their total cost of goods that they are willing to pay a higher price for it.

Concept 3: Customer-centric Segmentation Is Not Just the Same as Segmenting Customers?

When we talk of customer-centric segmentation, we want to draw attention to the fact that we are not using the phrase 'customer segmentation'. We are not suggesting that *customers* (people or organizations), be segmented (divided into different groups) based on their needs. This would be very simplistic, since it assumes that each organization or individual would have the same needs for all consumption or purchase situations even with respect to the same product category, let alone across product categories. For instance, a company may need international compatibility in the word processing and analytics software used by its executives dealing with overseas suppliers and hence buy the latest upgrades, and *yet* be quite behind the times in the software used by certain sections of the administrative staff. In the retail business, customer needs and buying behaviour change according to the kind of items being bought. In biscuits, depending on the time of the day or the occasion of consumption, the needs that a biscuit has to fulfil would be quite different. Therefore, we urge that strategists be precise and explicit and talk and think about *customer variables*-based segmentation (of usage occasions, or money spent, etc.).

Concept 4: How about Using Key Buying Factors or Product Attributes Preferred as a Basis to Segment the Market?

Often we find that strategy consultants advise their clients to identify market segments based on *key buying factors* or a ranking of product attributes that customers desire. In order to find this, surveys are conducted that establish how many customers want 45 HP and above tractors, and are not particularly concerned about warranty period, how many are *service intensive* in their desires, and so on. Segmenting the market universe this way is no better than product segmentation, and just as unstable and limited. The *motorcycle preferrer–scooter rejecter* segment of people have been known to be the first to switch when a new scooter offering style and many 'show-off' features is launched, especially if these were the two reasons why they preferred a motorcycle to begin with. Not only are such key buying factors or product attribute preferences-based segments unstable when new competition comes in and upsets status quo with *never before* benefits and prices, they are also not homogeneous.

'*Strong tea*' *preferrers* is a segment that is often identified based on key buying factors (Do you prefer strong tea or flavoured mild tea?) However, these people could include those whose need is to stay awake late at night after a full meal (tea as a source of caffeine, but not stomach filling), as well as those who need a hunger-assuaging liquid snack

151

and use it as a medium to consume milk and sugar. These are different 'value spaces' and need different product and business design.

We often assume that the importance of a need and propensity to buy a product or a product attribute are the same. It is true that product-feature preferences can be, and often are, a signal of the underlying consumer needs, but for the purposes of business-market strategy, we feel that this is a limiting assumption.

People who want to buy small tractors are not people who are happy with less HP. They could be people with large farms who would like high efficiency, but cannot afford a larger tractor; or they could be people on whose farm size a larger tractor does not work. The strategic possibilities that this opens up for a farm equipment business may or may not include tractors at all. It is certainly true that motorcycle buyers in the Himalayan mountains seek different benefits from their vehicle than motorcycle buyers in Kerala who travel long distances in the plains. However, the point we would like to emphasize is that it is not the motorcycles preferences that are different, but the transportation needs that are different, given the different terrain and weather conditions (and perhaps even occupations). These transportation requirements are being served by a motorcycle with specific features (currently) and could be served better through segmentation based on terrain types and their requirements and motorcycles specially designed for these. However, if one were to work with the basic needs, the answer to this problem tomorrow could be a low-cost second-hand jeep with an affordable EMI, or a group transportation service, or a new type of two-wheeler altogether!

Concept 5: How about Business-Market Segmentation Based on Customer Behaviour with Respect to the Category?

Segmenting markets based on *what* people do is less useful and valuable than segmenting them on *why* they do it. Merely having *off-average* behaviour patterns is not a good enough basis for being considered a segment of strategic value. The question is, does this *off-average* behaviour signal a distinctive need? People who sleep for eight to ten hours every night versus those who sleep four to five hours could merely reflect different body constitutions, or could reflect sleep disorders that impair some people far more than they impair others. The needs arising out of the consequence of how much they sleep needs to be discovered before the market can be segmented along this variable. Therefore, we believe that behaviour is a very valuable clue in helping to discover interesting need segments and is the starting point for market segmentation but not the end point of it. The root cause that drives people to behave the way they do is a far better basis for business-market segmentation.

Concept 6: Drilling Down to the 'Root Cause' and Using It as a Basis for Business-Market Segmentation

There is a fundamental consumer reason or a root cause as to *why* they want something (key buying factors) or do something (buying behaviour observed), and it needs to be understood before blindly using preferences or behaviour as segmenting variables. For instance, people using a chartered accountant (CA) to file tax returns could actually be three segments, not one, if you do a root cause analysis. Some of us want our tax returns filed painlessly, and therefore we

153

outsource this task to a CA, because we are busy and believe that our time has better use somewhere else and is monetarily more valuable than the money we spend in paying the CA. Others may want to use a CA to file tax returns because they want to avail of every loophole or leeway in the tax laws, and want someone to defend them if the tax officer has queries on the income tax returns. This people-benefit root-cause method of market segmentation ensures that sloppy, low-value-creating segmentation like *uses CA to file taxes* or *does not use CA* does not happen. The same logic can be applied to the segment of people who do not use a CA. They could be those who have very simple tax returns and hence do not use a CA (for example, salaried employees with no other source of income), or those who do not trust a CA to keep their tax details or find them too expensive even though their tax filing needs complex handling. If you are marketing software products to help make tax paperwork easier, then lumping *everyone who uses a CA* (or does not use a CA) as a single segment to be targeted with a single product and a single marketing strategy does not make sound strategic sense.

Concept 7: What about Business-Market Segmentation Based on Geography (Urban versus Rural Markets, Western versus ASEAN Markets)?

Companies often talk in terms of rural and urban market segments. However, *rural* by itself is not a customer variable—it is a shorthand code or a proxy in the minds of strategy developers to mean *people who live in rural areas*. This does not mean very much because there is a lot of divergence in how rural people live, think and what they need. If the *intra-segment variance* of rural markets

154

is high, then this becomes a meaningless basis for market segmentation (for example, in Tamil Nadu, rural dwellers are better educated and more urban-connected and urban-like than rural people in Bihar; within a rural area, there are many different kinds of 'villagers', ranging from the rich landowners with children in the city to the young man who commutes to work in the nearest town, as well as the landless agricultural labourer). Segmenting the rural market for consumer durables, we may identify a high-value *urban* consumer segment comprising rural dwellers who are posted there in the course of their work but are urban in origin, as well as rural dwellers who work in the nearest urban town.

In the classic case we teach our class on Komatsu and Caterpillar, the industry segmentation *developed and developing markets* are shorthand code words for those markets which are past the stage of Level 1 infrastructure and those which are still in the first stage, where the government is the primary buyer, where price negotiation and corruption levels are high, and so on. Brazil, Russia, India and China (BRIC) or emerging markets are seen to be a single segment by several global companies. However, on many counts, nothing could be more different than these. The intra-segment variance is very high if you are a real businessman and not an economist. For example, if you are a youth marketer, then you will see that the gen-next in single-child China is quite different from that in large/extended-family India or the very westernized Brazil.

Concept 8: Needs, Benefits, and Value Spaces—Are They the Same Thing?

The words *needs* and *benefits* are often used quite interchangeably. However, benefits are what products offer and needs are what customers have. After our discussion in this chapter on consumer needs being different from product benefits desired, we would suggest removing the phrase *benefit segment* from the strategist's lexicon. Between *needs* and *value spaces*, we prefer the use of the word *value space*, because *needs* usually lead us down the path of consumers' recognizing and articulating what they need. *Value space* leads us even deeper into consumer or customer territory: what does the *need* stem from or arise from? What is the fundamental purpose why he uses a product? Benefit laddering theory talks of product features resulting in *benefits* or consequences that customers get. These benefits or consequences, in turn lead to the values that people are looking for.

For instances Fair and Lovely is trying to go well beyond the product attribute of 'disperses melanin' to the consequence that it 'makes you look fairer, prettier' to the value of 'enables you to make the most of what you have' on to the value of 'empowers you to seize and achieve'. Were it a business unit, then it is easy to see that if it does indeed occupy any of the latter two value spaces, then its *where to compete* playground is clear and offers multiple avenues for growth through new products and services.

To take an example of value spaces in banking, when it comes to money, women in dual-income households see themselves as nurturers and spend and save differently from men who see themselves as providers. Therefore, the value spaces that men and women seek from a private wealth manager are quite different.

Talking to customers about why they choose the ice cream that they do on different occasions, we discover interesting value spaces based on who the consumer is. The young ones say eating ice cream is akin to *rebellion*— thumb your nose at mom and do what you like and she disapproves of. The slightly older ones are looking for the value space of *greedy stomach fill pleasure at the lowest possible cost*. Teenagers and young adults talk of ice cream being in the value space of *mood elevator* or *freak-out indulgence*— of being the social means to *impress girlfriends*. We found a behaviour segment of married people who took a walk late at night, after dinner, to eat ice cream and clearly were in the value space of *evening intimacy and relaxation*, away from all the cares at home.

Again, the value spaces for coffee are *relaxation* and *stimulation*, and also a social symbol of a *power drink*. In fact, in south India, coffee is a humanizer and comfort food of a very basic nature. In north India, this value space is occupied by tea, and coffee is a hot beverage. When it comes to money, the value spaces are not really as prosaic as risk/return/liquidity. Money, as we all know, has several emotional value spaces: controls others; buys friends, love and security; makes me a good provider; etc. In the mobile phone industry, Nokia thinks of the value spaces for a cell phone as about being *fashion*, *fun* and *entertainment*, about *productivity enhancement* and *about reward for arrival— gift yourself the privilege*.

Value spaces for alcohol are consumption as part of a *bonding* or *social ritual*, externally oriented *macho signalling*; using alcohol as a means of *forgetting—escape from tough life*; for celebration, *as a de-stresser*, as a means of attaining and enjoying a pleasant *high* and even *as a prop* for expressing sophistication and discernment either to oneself or to the world. It is easy to see that if each of these were treated as a separate business, they would have very different product strategies, margin profiles, competition, and need different value delivery systems.

We believe that thinking of *markets as comprising sub-markets made up of value spaces* is the ultimate best practice in developing customer-centred business strategy. Thinking in terms of *value spaces* enables us to recognize all other forms of competition that reside in the same space. Using the label *need* in our experience, somehow, narrows people's thinking to a particular product category and takes it closer to product-related benefits. Since business-market strategy is concerned with fundamental needs that are consumer intrinsic, we suggest using words like *need arena* or *value space* as a reminder not to slip into product thinking. Furthermore, consumers do not think in terms of *needs*—they think in terms of 'what adds value to me or what makes my life better'. This is yet another reason why we prefer the label value space.

In the rest of this chapter, we discuss some case examples of business-market segmentation, both in B2B and B2C businesses, which illustrate some of the concepts we have outlined in this chapter.

Case Example: Business-Market Segmentation of a Paperboard Manufacturer

BC Paper (name disguised) was a company making high-quality duplex boards for packaging applications. They were nearing the limit of their production capacity. The decision, therefore, was whether to invest in new capacity or to modify some of their existing machines to deliver an increase in capacity. The concern was that since capacity in this business gets added in large chunks, any drop in market demand could severely impact the financial health of the company after the new capacity was invested in. The chairman of the company was absolutely clear that he did not want to play a volume game like some of his competitors, who were flooding the market with lower-quality duplex boards at lower prices. At the same time the question was: 'Would the market for benefit-sensitive duplex board consumption (that is, willing to pay a higher price for higher benefits) be large enough to support the new capacity?' The MD articulated the problem as follows:

> When I see the big FMCG companies building huge factories in the free trade zone to service exports to the USSR, I sometimes worry what will happen if exports to Russia fall for some reason. Also a lot of our duplex board goes into cigarette packaging and into packaging for match boxes. Last year, winter was mild and so traditional consumption of match boxes in the hilly areas (to light fires) declined quite sharply. And we all know that with cigarettes, depending on which way the government sets the excise duty each year, there are huge brands that just disappear. Take for example the mega brand called Charms, which was a big consumer of our board. It just disappeared when the government in its annual budget announcements changed the basis of computing duty from the size of the stick to *ad valorem*. Finally, we know that when times are hard, the two things that get under the scanner and get cut first are advertising and packaging. So can you tell me what demand will be? And can we afford to say 'no second quality at cheaper price'? Will the market for our kind of quality, at our kind of prices, be safe and will it continue to grow to support our new capacity?

What started off as a simple demand forecasting problem of the current and future market for each end use application, which would help decided whether to invest in new capacity or augment old capacity, actually was a market segmentation problem based on customer variables. The question being asked was: 'Are there enough segments of demand which will support our chosen *how to compete* of creating value advantage over competition by offering higher B and higher C?' We started by asking: 'What would make customers pay a higher B and a higher C?' The answer was that those that had specific functional requirements—like marine product exporters who needed to store their packed goods in chill rooms and needed packaging that was fungus-resistant, moisture-proof and so on—were willing to pay more for these benefits than those who needed better aesthetics for their brands given their value creation strategy for their end consumers.

We then did a round of qualitative conversations with customers to understand how they thought about when to cut packaging and when not to. The results were that every customer company that was a consumer of duplex boards had certain brands for which it would hang in there and not cut packaging quality unless pushed to a wall, and certain brands for which it would proactively cut packaging quality in order to release cash. They would deal with the rest of the consumption on a case by case, wait-and-watch basis.

Taking all these into account, we designed a business-market segmentation plan for duplex board tonnage: we defined the market universe as the total tonnage of duplex board consumed, then we fashioned various knives made of relevant customer variables to cut up the market universe in a way that would create the desired value advantage for the company. Figure 7.1 displays this final segmentation scheme. All end-use applications were divided—based on customer interviews, not company conjecture—into *stable* and *unstable*. Exports to Russia were unstable, as were cigarette, liquor, matchboxes and parts of the gems and jewellery export consumption of those customers who did not own their own customers, but were selling in the wholesale market, and were wholly dependent on the middleman. They were further divided into whether the purpose of using duplex board was for aesthetic or functional reasons, and later we further segmented them into those for whom the aesthetic benefit was *mission critical*, like jewellery exporters where the card, on which the jewellery was displayed and placed, needed to be of a

Figure 7.2: Segmentation of Paperboard Tonnage

End use → Quality attitude ↓	Stable end-use		Unstable end-use	
	Functional	Aesthetic	Functional	Aesthetic
Will hang in there unless pushed to a wall	* Most attractive segment	*	*	*
Will proactively cut costs at first sign of trouble	*	*	*	* Least attractive segment
Rest	*	*	*	

Note: Data to be obtained for each cell: list of end uses/end users; total tonnage in the segment, share by end use; market shares of the paperboard company and its competitors.

very high *mirror board* quality, and those for whom it was a frill more than a necessity, like cartons for cough syrup bottles that were needed merely to make them stand out a bit on the chemist shelf (though brand choice was usually made based on a doctor's recommendation).

Customers were further asked for which of their end-use applications they would decide to hang in there preserving quality, unless pushed to the wall, and for which ones would they proactively cut quality, the minute the environment looked tough. Interestingly, and counter-intuitively, most said that they would cut quality at the first sign of margin pressure for their big market share brands, which had solid customer loyalty, but hang in there for their niche premium brands.

The final computation of paper board tonnage in each cell was done based on census interviews with large end users and sample interviews with appropriately selected small users in each end-user category. Once we had the segmentation of paper board tonnage, we were able to map for each cell, what the end-user industry composition was, for which exact end uses and what the market share of BC Paperboard and each competitor was. We found that the company had almost 90 per cent market share in the most attractive segment of applications: the functional benefits sought and will hang in there and not debase packaging quality unless pushed to the wall. The tonnage in the segments of *unstable–aesthetic needs–will proactively cut cost* was where the *unorganized sector* players of paperboard were playing. Based on the results of this, the *where to compete* was determined after analysis of *pain–gain* offered by each cell and the implications for *how to compete*. Only then was the choice between expanding capacity with new machines versus just augmenting existing machines made.

BUSINESS-MARKET SEGMENTATION BASED ON MACRO CONSUMER TRENDS

Broader social trends change consumer needs and value spaces for a variety of businesses and offer avenues for innovatively cutting up markets or identifying high-value oases ahead of competition. The rise of a distinctive new generation or a distinctive age cohort, who have had a set of shared experiences that shape their worldview and makes it different from others, provides a unique *where to compete* opportunity. Liberalization children who are India's first capitalist free market generation is one example. As they go through different phases of their lives, they form distinctive segments—as teenagers, as householders etc. The breakdown of the joint family, the rise of independent women moving away from traditional roles, the rise of the Indian multinational, that is, Indian companies going global, and so on. One of our clients, an investment banker, watched the increase in the number of Indian companies who had entered early in the liberalization game into joint ventures with foreign partners and then broke up, and he concluded that there was an interesting value space for the 'divorce lawyer' equivalent in his business.

Colgate Palmolive's oral care business in India, its main business, owned over 60 per cent of the Indian toothpaste market. Its *where to compete* market strategy was to treat the entire market as a single segment and it's *how to compete* was to offer them a single catch-all value proposition of 'stops bad breath and fights tooth decay', delivered through a single product (Colgate Dental Cream), designed for the 'average' customer. Hindustan Unilever's (HUL) newly set up oral care business chose its *where to compete* strategy based on the insight that there was a

163

growing consumer segment of more affluent or better-educated mothers of children who understood the gravity of tooth decay in children, took their kids for regular dental check-ups, and were *more-than-average* concerned about it. HUL decided to compete with a very high intensity in this sub-market, with a rivalry proposition of advanced germ kill, backed by scientific ingredients and wrested a chunk of this sub-market of customers successfully from Colgate. What is more important was that they managed to establish themselves with current and potential (Colgate) customers as providers of modern, scientific and advanced oral care for their children's precious teeth and well-being. This laid the foundation that enabled them to potentially extend their tentacles deep into a high-value market (customer) segment, which is far more benefit sensitive than it is price sensitive. It also potentially laid the foundations for people to want to *graduate to better* when they got more affluent, more educated—and, hence, secured the future for their business.

Case example: Business-Market Segmentation for a Tractor Manufacturer

To consider a different example: Tractors India (real name changed) was a very successful company that marketed and manufactured tractors. The company thought of their market as *the tractor market* and their customer as *the potential buyer of tractors*. To begin with, this product-centric view of the world is totally limiting for a growth-oriented company that has a deep and distinctive distribution in rural India to its advantage and a brand name that is known and trusted by Indian farmers. Only about 10 per cent of farms in India are of a size where the purchase of a tractor is economically justified, and over half the farms are of a size where it is not even possible to physically use a tractor. Therefore, defining themselves only in terms of the tractor market and not the *farmer* market had shut off avenues of growth which could have been explored by mechanizing small farms in several ways with the use of implements like power tillers, sprayers, motorized hoes, and so on. Their market universe should have been defined in a customer-based way, focusing on the farmers instead of the tractors!

Even within the tractor market, as they defined it, they further segmented it based on HP or the tractor bought. It was common to hear talk of 'John Deere will come in at the >45 HP segment of the market, or the <25–35 HP segment.' This was the basis for the *where to compete* decision. When new competitors came into the market and entered all HP segments, Tractors India felt that a better segmentation of the market was needed in order for them to retain competitive advantage. They felt intuitively that a portfolio of brands, each having its own HP range, but targeting a different market segment, may be the way to go. The existing HP-based segmentation was not good enough because all players were competing or eventually intending to compete in all segments. Furthermore, the end consumer prices of the products at this point were somewhat distorted owing to the somewhat illogical and differential excise duty on different sizes of products—as soon as these illogical duty structures would change, the market would *shift* again.

Segmenting the market by the type of crop grown and designing tractors for rice or wheat was again seen to be not sensible because multi-cropping was increasing in the country. Furthermore, even if the crop's growth was intimately related to the soil conditions that the tractors had to perform in, the new generation of tractors entering the market were capable of functioning in all soil conditions. Segmenting the market on key buying factors or attachments required or even on financing needs, again, was seen to offer no real strategic advantage. We spoke to the farmers at length about tractors, but succeeded in making very little breakthrough in finding a segmenting scheme that was stable and would offer competitive advantage. At this point, some smart qualitative researchers decided to talk to farmers about farming and their farms rather than about tractors, and then the breakthrough occurred.

There emerged four kinds of farmer segments based on how they thought about and managed their farms:

1. **The ROI farmer:** He is the one who thought of his farm as a business and managed it as a business and thought of farm implements and tractors as investments that had the capability to yield superior returns to him. It was not so obvious that several small farmers would be included in this group, but clearly as crops like organic vegetables and herbs came to be demanded by new boutique retail chains that were mushrooming all over the country, even small farmers were thinking in the terms of return on investment (ROI).

2. **The cost–benefit balancing value optimizer:** Several farmers did want to maximize the revenue that their farms could give them, but did not want to borrow and invest a whole lot of money in making this happen. To them, the risk of borrowing for a business subject to nature's vagaries was too daunting. Therefore, on a case-by-case basis they looked at investments in their farms and were often willing to settle for investing in things that saved them a lower benefit, but at a lower cost.

166

3. **The cash-flow minimizer:** Typically a small farmer, he wanted to minimize cash outflow and manage within whatever income his farm gave him with the bare minimum input. Typically, he preferred to custom hire farm equipment rather than invest in buying his own.
4. **The bullock cart user:** This farmer was still in the primitive age as far as his farm was concerned and had very little money. Any mechanical devices were most welcome.

The company then decided to target a range of products and services designed based on the extra sums at each segment for these investors. The ROI farmer was offered a range of implements that could ride on a tractor, online price discovery, and transaction assistance, on specialized agricultural inputs to maximize yields, contract farming opportunities for export-oriented fruits and vegetables, and so on. The optimizer meanwhile was offered a range of tractors, with options for the more regular-use implements, basic yield improvement input packages like seed and fertilizer, and simple price discovery mechanisms.

The company is now actively engaged in looking at the cash flow minimizer and bullock car user and exploring offering a range of implements and tractors and other mechanical tools offered on a rentable basis.

Case example: Water Treatment Equipment

To stay with the example of the water treatment unit, one of the companies we know in this space used to historically segment its customers using the customer variable of heavy, medium, light industry. Therefore, they had historically focused on *heavy* industry, which was synonymous with large, complex plants requiring large water treatment plants with a high degree of customization and hence a very lucrative and high-value market segment. Customers belonging to *medium* and *light* industry were not seen to be very attractive customer segments because they were small companies and not very sophisticated, and they bought low-priced non-customized solutions. Further, in the days of India's controlled economy, most heavy-industry customers were from the public sector, and hence the company's selling methods were all geared to serving the public sector. The company continued to work with this segmentation even though the customer world around it changed as India's economy got decontrolled. By not re-examining this segmentation logic and paradigm, they started losing out on the new private sector entrants into *heavy industry* because they were geared to public sector behaviour and norms. They also did not notice the relative decline of the public sector, and how they were no longer cutting-edge *lighthouse* customers to have and learn from. They also lost out to competition who had capitalized on the several new sophisticated *medium* and *light* manufacturing units that had come into existence. These were export-oriented auto component units, pharmaceutical and textile processing companies, etc., who needed to improve their manufacturing efficiencies and processes in order to successfully compete globally; they also assumed that *light* manufacturing businesses did not require any customization, although, in fact, these businesses operated with non-standard plants that had grown bit by bit, over time, and needed customization quite desperately. Overall, their failure to segment their market according to customer variables cost them heavily.

Case example: Biscuits

The MD of one of India's leading biscuit companies narrates the story of how their company was once content to describe their market universe as those consuming biscuits. Since the consumption of biscuits was almost entirely at home, the market universe they thought about was people *eating biscuits at home*. They then segmented their market by product type: glucose biscuits, digestive biscuits, cream biscuits, crackers, savouries, etc. Their fight with their competition was entirely product based—glucose versus non-glucose, digestive versus digestive, etc. Creating customer perceived value advantage was expectedly tough as the average quality of the staple biscuits available in the market improved. Market share increases were hard to pull off for the company, and, therefore, growing faster than competition, and faster than the market average, was tough.

The MD in question decided to re-segment the market to the advantage of their own company (and the disadvantage of others) by using more sophisticated *need-arena*-based segmentation. They did, however, make an exception to this and carved out a demographics-based segment of *children eating biscuits*. While this did not quite fit a need arena, it defined an interesting, valuable, and growing consumer segment—children—and provided enough differentiated opportunities in terms of *how to compete*. They already had a strong brand presence in this user group and could easily build on this. Apart from this, they could also build serious competitive advantage by doing school-based programmes, having exciting shapes and packaging, forming alliances with other non-conflict businesses addressing children, and so on. They felt that they would be able to do this far better than any competitor because they had superior customer insight into this target group, as well as more sophisticated branding and marketing skills which could help them build an emotional value advantage. *Healthy snacking*, or people who were looking at healthier options for their hunger snacking or boredom snacking, was a need-arena-based segment that they defined. *Sheer indulgence* was another need-arena-based segment, which was about pampering your palate and feeling rich and taken care of. Serve *with pride–guest interface* was yet another need-arena-based segment. She also looked at the consumption arena and decided that each time slot for eating could be an interesting segment served with a separate biscuit option, which would highlight a need and associate a time slot with it. Again, we want to point out that all the segmentation variables used here are customer-based, not product-based.

However, all this was still tightly within the confines of the *current biscuit market*, which was mostly about for-home buying and at-home consumption, with perhaps the slight exception of children's snack boxes for school. As they studied the market, they noticed that in recent years there had been a change in Indian lifestyles, which resulted in an increase in eating out-of-home—in movie theatres, at malls, at airports, at street corners. This was driven partly by the lifestyle changes that a growth economy forces and partly by the availability of interesting options like boiled corn, dim sums, curd rice packs, sandwiches and several smart new options that were now available out of home. Looking at it through the *people* and *eating* lens, it became clear that there was an entire market out there that biscuits were not a part of (just as SWA discovered an interesting travel market that air travel was not a part of). Could it become part of the

170

company's served market? In what shape and form could value advantage be created over competition? Would the company have to change the game it played, more radically, or should it stay out of this part of the *share of stomachs* altogether?

The *market universe* in the case of people eating out of home could either be defined as the 'ice cream' market or the 'dim sum' market or the 'sandwich' market, if one were to approach this in product–market terms. However, in customer-centred terms, people spending money on snacking and eating at various places on various occasions for various reasons was the market universe. The MD chose to smartly define the company's market universe as being in-between snacking and eating and the segment they chose to carve was *eating in-between meals*. Ideally, this universe should be segmented into the benefits sought: hunger control, boredom, fun, social interface. However, they chose a mainstream across-the-board *benefit arena*—healthier snacking (healthier compared to other options, that is). Clearly, their universe was *health-conscious snacker*, which, they figured, was more or less everyone in today's world.

With this approach of customer-based market segmentation to defining their *where to compete* choices, they managed to get the company to play in a broader set of playgrounds than it originally would have, had it stayed within the 'biscuit market' boundary; and created competitive advantage by changing the rules of the game and forcing competition to follow suit. By creating sharp value delivery systems (as discussed in Chapter 6) for each chosen segment, they further managed to lock competition out for long enough to reap the brand benefits of being 'new and different'.

Case example: Restaurants

After all this discussion, it is easy to see why product segments, despite being so popular with strategists, do not always offer strategic value—because they fail to reflect segments or pockets of distinctive needs and do not adequately protect the company against disruptive competitor activity, which changes the rules of how the game is played in the market. At a holiday resort, for instance, the owners might think of their food and beverage market as comprising two segments: à la carte and buffet. They have a mental model that says buffet meals are what *average* resort guests usually eat while *à la carte* is for those guests who want a fine dining experience and are willing to pay more for it and want to choose their menu. In reality, the *à la carte* comprises two different kinds of resort guests: those who indeed want the fine dining experience and those who feel that paying for two dishes on the *à la carte* menu is cheaper than paying for the buffet. Therefore, unlike a product-based segmentation, which has too much intra-segment variance, a people-based segmentation to reflect different fundamental needs would be *economy seekers, mainstream fun dining variety seekers* and *convenience and 'no fuss' seekers*. All of them want an exceptional quality of food. The strategic possibilities with this segmentation scheme—extracting value from consumers by delivering value to them and managing the company's cost—are enormous. Economy seekers could be encouraged to do part buffets (like soup, salad and one non-vegetarian dish) or do takeaways that can be consumed somewhere with a glorious view. Fine dining on the other hand, unfettered by the economy cushions, can be a place where people dress up for a great dining experience and celebrate or romance. Fun dining variety seekers and 'convenience and no-fuss' seekers can be served through a range of regular buffet items. Similarly, instant coffee, specially brewed coffee and flavoured coffees offer more strategic confusion than value. People who drink coffee for relaxation, for stimulation (caffeine kick), for socialization or for indulgence are strategically far more valuable segment definitions with a whole set of business discussions that go with each. It is important to note that diners or coffee drinkers may be different things at different time. Therefore, it is not just *people*, but also *people–eating,* or *people–coffee drinking;* these are categories that we use to define the market, and that is what we further divide into sub-markets.

CHAPTER 8

Consumer Insight for Shaping Business Strategy

Thus far, we have repeatedly pointed to the importance of consumer/ customer insight to achieve a winning business strategy. We have designated as the 'front end' or the engine of business strategy, the business-market strategy, which defines where and how a business chooses to play in the market: which playgrounds or parts of the market the company chooses to play in, what game it chooses to play in each, and what special rivalry propositions or ways of playing it chooses in order to win. We have repeatedly stated that business-market strategy should not be based on products, prices and supplier-side variables, but on consumer needs and value spaces, and value packages that provide consumer-perceived value advantage over competition. We are invariably asked how such consumer (or customer) insight can be obtained, and we are told many stories about how market research fails to step up to the line and deliver.

This chapter discusses some interesting mindsets and approaches, methodologies, tools and frameworks to obtain consumer insight relevant for business strategy. Since a

Figure 8.1: The CBBS Framework: Customer Insight

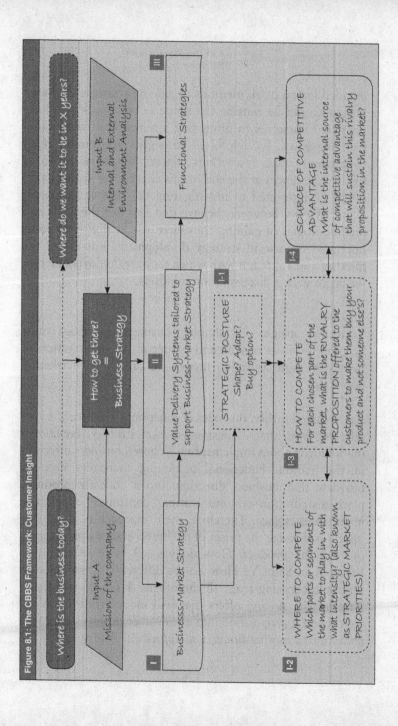

detailed listing of all methods of gaining strategic customer insight would be outside the scope of this book, we have restricted ourselves to discussing a selection of topics that we believe will be helpful to strategists and enable them to guide market researchers better. We have provided further references at the end of this chapter for readers who might be interested in investigating the subject in greater detail. We do, however, believe that it is not the tools and methodologies of gaining consumer insight that need to be upgraded for use in strategy development, but rather the mindset and approach with which they are deployed. Hence, we begin with a discussion on mindsets.

Mindset

Consumer insight for shaping business directions must be broader in its canvas and bolder in its investigation of 'why not' than consumer insight for functional marketing decisions.

As explained earlier, the focus of functional marketing is very different from that of business-market strategy. Functional marketing is about implementing a chosen business direction in the market. Functional marketing managers need to translate that business direction into a concrete product–price–distribution–communication consumer experience in the marketplace. Therefore, their approach to consumer insight is through the prism of the brand and/or the category, or even the product. How do we sell more of shampoo Brand X in State Y? How do we differentiate our telecom service advertising from all the others? How do we design introductory pricing offers that will induce trial? How do we convert a proposition into a consumer promise (*cheaper–better* into a *mother-in-law will approve*!)? And so on.

In contrast, the business strategist's job is to design the business-market strategy (or the front end of business strategy) and address questions such as 'how do we grow this business', and explore answers, which would include any of the following:

'Choose directions of growth which are step outs from the current product category/customer segments that the business operates in today', or 'What is the battlefront on which we should be engaging competition: Price? Product features? Service? Ease of distribution?' Or 'Which value spaces should we be playing in, and which should we stay out of, given our business mission?' Or 'How do we build sustained advantage over competition?' Or 'How should we de-risk the business from changes that will occur in the world of customers as a result on environmental or competitor strategy changes?' Or 'Are there any big opportunities that could arise as a result of environmental changes, which we can grab?' To answer these questions, strategic consumer insight is needed, and should be obtained by viewing markets through a lens of strategic possibilities, hence, be far more 'naïve' and open in its investigation and study an entire need arena, not merely a product- market, as functional marketing is wont to do (for example, study need for entertainment, not stay restricted to the digital music category).

Approach
Stay away from analytical tools to begin with, until you have robust consumer insight hypotheses.

We caution against *outsourcing* acquiring consumer insight to analytical tools like conjoint analysis (which provides a measurement of how consumers trade-off between different elements of a product offer), or cluster analysis (which asks consumers to rate different need dimensions on how much they want each and then group consumers into different clusters or segments based on their need patterns), or Kano analysis, borrowed from Quality Function Deployment (QFD), which identifies product features that, when improved on, can provide better value to customers than competition. The reason is that using all these tools requires some going-in hypothesis or pre-judgement about the dimensions along which customers make choices; therefore, many analytical tools end up providing better ways to play the game *within* the sandbox in which the game is currently already being played by competitors. The mission and purpose of strategy, however, is to find new and fresh ways to redefine the game itself, and not to play it a little bit better than the way others are playing it.

In our experience, consumer insight capable of driving strategic breakthroughs come from *naïve listening* to customers; not through the lens of the current business but through the lens of their needs, by broad and holistic understanding of a need arena (like transportation) rather than a narrow category (like motorcycles or cars).

Methodology

How should we map markets in a way that helps to 'see what no one else has seen (or bothered to notice) and think what no one else has about that which everybody sees?'

The *romantic* mode of strategy formulation is usually about newness and uncharted territory, and abounds with phrases and ideas like 'creating industry revolution', 'discovering new markets', 'being a shaper rather than an adaptor', 'blue ocean strategy', and so on. However, the *operating* or *classic* mode is where the problem lies, even in market-research-rich companies. This is not because the data is not available, but because the way in which it is analysed and synthesized does not tell the story of strategic market opportunity. The data is too often generated by looking at the market through the prism of the category of product or service the firm is engaged in. We suggest abandoning the product lens altogether and looking at the market as a collection of people who have a need. Again, a *need* segment is not to be confused with a *group of people buying Product X*. We prefer using the phrase *need arena* because it frames a certain *where to compete* playground, and because the word 'segment' has been overused to the extent of losing its clarity and sharpness.

Within the need arena, the most basic and most helpful analyses, often unavailable with strategists, are around market structure and consumer behaviour. The former provides inputs into where to compete, the latter into both where and how to compete.

Constructing strategic market structure maps

A strategic market structure map for a business of health food drinks used as milk additives should start with all people in the universe who could possibly consume this, and not start with all buyers or potential buyers of health food drinks. A strategic market structure map would then tell you how many people in this market (and who they are) have a felt need for additional nutrition or better still for the benefits or values that such nutrition can provide. How many—and who are they—want brain boosting (not brain boosters, which is a product; but brain boosting which is a benefit), how many worry about keeping bones intact in old age, how many want children to grow tall, how many do not worry about any such thing at all, how many are truly not bothered or concerned about anything, etc. For each such group, what are all the ways in which people do or do not fulfil that need, could be hanging from trees to grow tall, could be doing Sudoku to boost the brain, could be eating *badams* (almonds), could be taking multivitamin pills or even consuming health food/drinks. It has to answer the question of '*What are middle-aged, low-income folk doing to improve their health and fitness levels?*', rather than answer the question of '*What is the profile of consumers of health food drink used as milk additives?*' The latter starts with the product, the former with people. This often does not require a whole new approach. It may just require the way the percentages are calculated to be flipped around (that is, how many middle-aged low-income people drink health drinks may yield an answer of 3 per cent, but how many health drink consumers are middle aged and low income, may yield an answer of 33 per cent!). The fresh insight gained from looking at what else the middle-aged low-income consumers consume/do to stay healthy may be invaluable in shaping the business direction of the health food business.

In a much-celebrated case like that of SWA, as we discussed in Chapter 7, with such a people-travel map, it is possible to identify a large number of people who drive short hauls inter-city by car frequently, and to profile them and discover that they are business travellers. The next part is to *think what no one else has thought* about this traveller group or segment. The traditional supply-side adapter strategist will say that they do not form the airline market because it is cheaper and better for them to drive, thus describing '*what is*' and '*why it is so*'. But the customer-based strategist who believes in shaping markets could potentially see it as an opportunity to gain by offering better value to customer than their existing option: cut time, same cost, new kind of travel (air travel) option.

Karsanbhai Patel of Nirma did a similar thing. He looked at the market through the consumers' clothes cleaning lens and saw many laundry soap users and asked: 'Why is it not possible to give all of them a detergent that works better than their soap, and at only a marginally higher price?' He built a business system that was capable of low-cost manufacture and distribution and designed an acceptable quality detergent powder and bar which, though inferior to Surf, the best detergent in the market, was superior to laundry soap and at almost the same price (and one-third the price of Surf).

The question often asked about such businesses which revolutionize industries is: 'Was it a stroke of genius to dream this up? Would market research ever have thrown up this idea?' Part of it stems from seeing what no one else sees, that is, viewing market structure from a universe of people and their needs and what they currently use to fulfil them, and not from a universe of product buyers and competition users; and part of it is also due to thinking what no one else thinks about that which everybody sees. As these cases highlight, it is indeed a rare businessperson—such as one with Karsanbhai Patel's vision—who can see a group of consumers doing something and ask: 'Can this be done better such that value can be added to the customer in a way that also creates profit for the company?' However, to begin with, without a customer-centric, holistic map of a need arena (formally or informally generated), all that would have been visible would have been just the tip of the iceberg: current (and perhaps very satisfied) users of Surf or users of other airlines.

For purposes of *where to compete* decisions, a holistic map of a need arena shows the real size and spaces of market opportunity. If the need arena is to look more beautiful, then vitamins consumed for overall glow of skin should also figure in the map. Similarly, a motorcycle company should construct a holistic map of transportation including new and used cars, two-wheelers of all kinds (used, new and borrowed too), bicycles, public transport and walking. In many cases, this information will exist in different matrices called the *bicycle market* or the *used car market*, but will not be synthesized into a single matrix. Thus, a two-wheeler company we worked for missed the fact that 60 per cent of car owners had two-wheelers too and had very specific uses for the two-wheelers—a nice *island of value* that could perhaps be exploited. Banks are perhaps the least holistic customer centric in this regard. They assume that customers think assets and liabilities, investments and debt in different silos of their mind when, in fact, they are actually making trade-offs between buying a second house or putting that money in the stock market.

After seeing holistic market maps of a need arena, companies are often surprised to find that they compete in less than 10 per cent of the need arena and with a lot more unlikely competitors. This entire discussion applies not just to consumer goods companies, but also to B2B companies— the need arena could be power saving, sustainability practices or level of automation. The tractor market in India, according to tractor manufacturers, is growing very slowly, is likely to get consolidated soon, and so on. Viewed through the lens of tractors, this is perhaps correct. But viewed in terms of a holistic market structure map that starts with the farmer, it will very soon become apparent that only a fraction of farmers (the large ones) own tractors or hire and use tractors. A *where to compete* customer-based view would urge tractor companies to look at farm mechanization (not necessarily through tractors) as their business playground Finally, market structure maps must be modelled to see what they could become in the next five years, given assumptions of demographic shift and supply-side events as well as natural economic growth. This will answer the most important question of: What will future customer of category XYZ that I compete in today look like? What new customers are coming into the market that I will miss out on? And so on.

Tool
Benefit Structure Analysis for constructing strategic market structure maps.

Our favourite inspiration on how to construct a strategic market structure map is from a paper called *Benefit Structure Analysis* by John Myers (1976). He recommends creation of an *n*-dimensional map based on a consumer/customer survey. The questions are as simple as: (a) What are the things that you cleaned in your house yesterday? Any more things cleaned in the past week? Any more in the past month? (b) For each of these cleaning occasions or events, tell me how often do you clean it, what do you use to clean, who cleans it, how much do you spend per occasion on cleaning it; and (c) To this we can then add a set of attitudes attached to each cleaning area in the respondent's mind: How painful do you find this? How happy are you with the results (measured as *how important* is this area being cleaned, in your overall cleaning regime as scored on a five-point 'importance' scale and how happy are you with the *performance* you achieve, again scored on a five-point 'happiness' scale)?

Myers describes the numerical value of 'importance score minus performance score' as a deficiency. This deficiency can be *positive* (performance score greater than importance score) or *negative* (importance score greater than performance score), both throwing up interesting opportunities for creating value advantage. He makes a valid point that with this *n*-dimensional map of behaver [(areas of cleaning, frequency, products used, who cleans, etc.) × attitude (painfulness, performance, importance) × money spent], created for a sample of representative people in the target universe, the analysis is limited only by the imagination of the user. It can be used to identify usage or attitude segments, sizes, and profile them and systematically point to areas of opportunity that are not obvious.

Of course, an alternative way to segment the market for household cleaning is to understand how the consumer thinks about *value spaces*: cleaning that makes me feel positive and vibrant, cleaning that keeps germs and diseases out of the household by sanitizing, cleaning that makes me ashamed or earns one compliments from guests, and so on. In crowded markets, both B2B and B2C, we would recommend a first-hand understanding of the customer-based picture of the market in terms of understanding the hard market structure and players in the different parts of the market. It also leads to rapid identification of opportunities for re- conceiving products and services, or redrawing boundaries or discovering opportunities for whole new markets to expand and create.

METHODOLOGY: UNDERSTANDING CONSUMER BEHAVIOUR

How to Identify Value Spaces

Simple naïve listening to customers or consumers about the context of their usage of products/services and the relevance of it in their lives quite easily and clearly leads to identifying need arenas or value spaces. For instance, asking consumers the where and how of consuming alcohol and the consideration for brand choice will tell you that alcohol operates in the value spaces (as we discussed in the previous chapter on segmentation as well) of bonding or social rituals, macho signalling, forgetting difficulties, an escape from life, etc. Asking people the simple question of what are the occasions or reasons that trigger the '*chai ho jai*' thought leads to discovering interesting value spaces of 'energizer' (like petrol in a car); 'humanizer' (I cannot start my day without it); 'the elevenses break' (reward for hard work); 'time pass' (chat sessions with friends); etc.

If each of these value spaces are thought of as a separate country or a distinct market (maybe with overlapping consumers, but on different consumption occasions), then the way to build consumer-perceived value advantage in each of these spaces would be quite different, as would be the way to actually deliver it. Marketing to the bonding/social rituals value space would require a much greater focus on bars, picnic spots, outdoor distribution, whereas marketing to the relaxation and distress relief value space must be home centred, and so on.

Similarly, talk to companies about their usage of IT and you will learn that they see *getting core processes running smoothly and efficiently* as a value space and *enabling personal productivity* as another space, *enabling top-line growth* as a meta value space, and *cutting operating costs* as another. Children will tell you that ice cream straddles many value spaces, from *mood elevation* to *extraction of indulgence* from mom. The same cell phone might be in the value space of *productivity improvement* for executives, *entertainment* for teenagers and *guilt minimizer* for women who have to leave their children at home. Finding such value spaces is not a problem—conversations with customers around the *when/how/for what do you use and where does it fit in your life* questions will yield them quite easily. The reason why companies do not want to build strategy further around this is that their organizations are often product-centric structures and they do not want to disrupt existing processes (see Chapter 6 on VDS).

HOW TO CREATE DISCONTINUOUS VALUE ADVANTAGE AND EXPLODING GROWTH: APPROACH OF 'BREAKING COMPROMISES'

Clients often ask: 'How can we differentiate in a crowded market? How do we create consumer-perceived value advantage in such markets? How do we know which innovations we do will "click" and which will not?' One methodology that we particularly like, and believe is hugely helpful in creating value advantage and winning rivalry propositions, is that of *breaking compromises* (Silverstein and Stalk 2000: 3). At its heart is the following logic:

> Most companies today are searching for growth. How and where should they look? One powerful way to grow is through innovations that break the fundamental 'compromises' of a business . . . breakaway growth can be the result.
>
> Compromises are concessions demanded of the consumer by most companies in an industry. They occur when the industry imposes its own operating constraints on customers. Usually customers accept these compromises as just the way the business works—inevitable trade-offs that have to be endured!

> But a compromise is different from a trade-off . . . no law of nature or economics decrees that hotel rooms can't be ready before late afternoon [check-in time 4 PM]. (Silverstein and Stalk 2000: 3)

Connecting this approach to our earlier discussion on acknowledging and accepting the obvious, we are saying that consumer areas of unhappy compromises are well known to us because consumers tell us so very often. Compromises are far bigger than pain points. They are the wistful: 'Doesn't everybody know that these are the rules of the game? I wish it weren't so!' We suggest plotting these compromises as in Figure 8.1 and then having the company ask itself what they can do to break this compromise.

To cite an example: Everybody knows that customers are unhappy about having to choose between mileage and power in a two-wheeler. Finally, Japanese innovation produced a 100 cc motorcycle that provided adequate power as well as superb mileage. As a result of this, India is now the second largest motorcycle market in the world, the scooter market was virtually extinguished and Hero Honda has experienced more than a decade of enviable

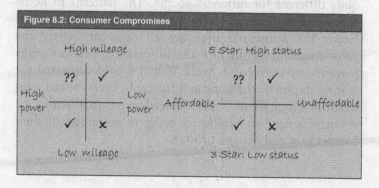

Figure 8.2: Consumer Compromises

187

growth. Nokia broke the compromise in the Indian market that low-price versions of phones would not have good styling, and now the consumer is forcing every category to follow suit.

Again, the hotel industry in India is forcing people to pay an arm and a leg for facilities that they do not use, just so that they can have a decent address that they can display when they meet new business prospects or customers who ask the apparently innocuous but loaded question: 'And where are you staying?' A new category of affordable hotels, priced like three-star hotels, but positioned and skilfully branded as a high-status sensible hotel, high on functionality, low on frills (wireless Internet in every room and in all common spaces, but no bathtub, jacuzzi or hairdresser; gym, but no swimming pool; two restaurants but not a whole range), will unlock huge value.

In the refrigerator business, companies often claim that there is not much anyone can do with a refrigerator—they will all look and perform the same. However, this argument is hard to swallow if we look at the refrigerator as a storage and preservation need arena. Shopping patterns, attitudes towards storing food—both fresh and leftover food—are quite different for different people. The patterns of home entertainment, eating, family structure, what sort of good *basket* the household uses are all different. Surely the value spaces, therefore, are also different, or product usage patterns are different as well. Would a cold cupboard for storing staples be the same as a freezer to keep cooked food fresh for a long time? These are need arenas that innovative companies need to explore in order to get ahead of their competition and expand growth.

Approach
Study end-to-end user experience in order to obtain superior value insight.

A mistake that companies often make in obtaining value insight is that they only study the area that they see as their core business, thus, not fully understanding the full gamut of needs the customer has, given the context in which he uses the product category in question and how and why he processes value and why. Therefore, they do not see low-hanging fruit opportunities to significantly improve the value of their offering. If getting to the airport is a battle because of terrible infrastructure and the crowded airport facilities, then having perfection from the minute of boarding the flight till landing does not add a great deal of value, especially if air traffic delays make journeys longer. It is in the context of this end-to-end experience that consumer value equations are built and value processing is done. Enough numbers of plug points at airline lounges to charge depleted mobile phones and free Wi-Fi may add far greater value than a free glass of champagne or extra entertainment on board. You may decide your own business boundaries of operation, but in the customer's world, how they process value within your boundary is influenced by the entire experience chain. Therefore, air-conditioner companies that can ensure quicker, hassle-free installation experience may add more value to customers than those that have a visibly superior product but do not offer to paint back the wall that they broke around the window in order to fit the air conditioner!

A related point in B2B businesses is to understand what the product becomes as it progresses along the chain to the end customer. A steel company we worked for used to convince us that 'steel is steel' no matter what you do. However, when we talked to his major supplier, a fasteners (nuts and bolts) manufacturer, he said: 'To them it's just a piece of steel. To me it is a wheel belt on a speeding truck on a highway and I am terrified that it may snap and lives will be lost.'

Approach
Adding value at the level of the 'augmented' product.

Theodore Levitt, the greatest guru of marketing, propounded the concept of the 'generic' product and the 'augmented' product. Philip Kotler's definition of the various levels of offers to consumers, based on Levitt's work, is that the *generic product is* a version of the product containing only those attributes or characteristics absolutely necessary for it to function (for example, core software); the *expected product* is the set of attributes or characteristics that buyers normally expect and agree to when they purchase a product (for example, software plus an operating manual + a recovery disk + a guarantee); and the *augmented product is* the inclusion of additional features, benefits, attributes or related services that serve to differentiate the product from its competitors (for example, self-diagnostic module, or automatic data backup facilities with antivirus software, and so on). Kotler notes that much of the competition occurs at the augmented product level (see http://www. provenmodels.com/16/five-product-levels/philip-kotler/).

In the parlance of our discussion thus far, it is about deciding what you can do around the product to improve the value by improving the user experience, about the services that are linked to how your customer can use and fit your product better in the scheme of his business or life.

Companies do not often study the entire usage context end-to-end and, hence, pass up opportunities for value advantage that are available at the level of the augmented product.

A chemical manufacturer we know mapped the entire context of usage of his customers of caustic soda, which, by all conventional wisdom, is a 'commodity'. There were opportunities to add value (by increasing 'B'enefit and decreasing 'C'ost) to use the concepts we discussed in Chapter 5 in the areas of transportation, storage and usage. He then investigated as to which customer (end use) segments were buying over-engineered better quality caustic soda and were happier to accept even lower quality at lower prices. The company also supplied sodium tripolyphosphate (STPP) to a large detergent producer. When they studied their new product development plans, they found the company debating how best to offer a detergent powder with big 'grains', which added consumer perceived value advantage to *their* consumer in *his* business. Would building a new spray drying unit be worth it? The chemicals company offered to create bigger STPP granules for them instead, at a price which proved to be financially beneficial for the chemicals company and the detergents producer.

As we have said often, B2B companies often only end up talking to their customers about their own business but not about their customers' business, thus losing opportunities for creating value advantage by helping your customer serve his customer better. Doctors would appreciate services from pharmaceutical companies like SMS alerts to patients for medication timing, and reminders about appointments, which would help improve compliance from patients, hence ensuring better recovery rates, and improve the doctor's reputation among the patients' community.

Mindset: Breaking the tyranny of the served-market.

A company making air conditioners decided that it had to grow through expanding the market for air conditioners in homes and small offices. They concluded that the number of people who had air-conditioned cars and not air-conditioned homes was large, and that there was a large potential opportunity for market expansion. They decided to get 'customer-centric' about air conditioners. The reason we have put the inverted commas in the previous sentence is that they decided to be 'customer-centric' about a product space and, thus, suffered from myopia. Surveys showed that air conditioner penetration is low even in Social Class A and B households (that is, the top 30 per cent income earners in urban India) because they are seen to be too expensive on the running costs, and people said they did not really feel the need. However, had the company looked at the consumer need of *heat control*—that is to say, the need arena of keeping the home cool in summer, they would have realized that the air cooler (the poor cousin of the air conditioner) had already penetrated 60 per cent of the Social Class A and B households. The task was not to get a cooling gadget into the home, but to fight a battle for value advantage with air coolers. And over the past few years, air coolers have got better in look, design and performance and even come window-mounted, exactly like air conditioners. What is more, their running costs are a lot lower every month as they consume very little electricity.

This then leads to the question of how to segment the market such that we could identify places where coolers do not work as well, thereby giving air conditioners a tangible Value = Benefit - Cost (V = B-C) advantage. The answer then is that in humid coastal areas, air coolers do not work well as they add to the humidity (hence the historical name for them—desert coolers). We therefore segmented the market based on potential for competitive advantage, into coastal areas of India and non-coastal areas of India and found out the relative population of Social Class A and B (that is, the top two social classes) households in each segment (more in non-coastal than coastal). In the strategic market prioritization, it was the coastal areas that were the highest priority market. Based on consumer investigation, we concluded that consumers did not want cooling that chilled them to the bone—they just wanted a comfortable temperature of 23 or 24 degree centigrade and were also willing to settle for less cooling and a lower-price, smaller-capacity air conditioner. In any case, in primary urban markets, bedrooms were quite small. Asking the question of 'how can we reduce running cost', we drew on a consumer comment that frequently surfaced: 'Can you not do what motorcycles do with fuel consumption? Give us the equivalent of the 100 km per litre breakthrough in electricity consumption'. The MD of the air conditioner company asked us, 'Isn't there a way to change the value processing algorithm that exists in people's minds, so that they can perceive the running costs to be lower? For example, most homes do not have heaters in winter in non-coastal areas where it gets very cold—so if we provided a heater-cum-air conditioner would we in some way be able to solve the running cost problem?'

We went back to the consumers, and using formal conjoint analysis, we understood how much value they attached to each level of benefit on each dimension and developed a value package around the proposition of *makes more sense to buy than an air cooler*. Similarly, we found that companies in the PC business and the PC software business kept monitoring the metric of PC penetration, and concluded that the market was not yet ready, not realizing the fact that mobile phones had become the point of access to the Internet and the PC was being bypassed totally.

Approach: Consumer insight for creating industry revolution.

Gary Hamel, in 'Strategy as Revolution' (1996), talks of three routes to leading an industry revolution, that could leave competitors far behind. These routes are: (a) re-conceiving products and services; (b) redrawing boundaries of categories; and (c) redefining market spaces (see Figure 8.2).

Though these are discussed in the context of business strategy by a business strategist, they actually define different ways of playing the game in the market, and bear out our view that market strategy and business strategy are truly intertwined.

In the first aspect of *re-conceiving products and services*, he suggests searching for new functionalities of existing forms (for example, smart cards to open doors in hotels, not just to use as credit cards), for new forms of existing functionalities (sanitizer rather than soap to clean hands), and to generally find breakthrough ways to improve rational and emotional value to the customer (Walkman, iPod, touchscreen photo viewer, etc.). Does this require customer insight or inventor smarts? The answer is that it requires inventor smarts, but the difference between inventions that succeed and those that do not is whether customers think they add value to their lives or not. A gadget that brilliantly automates a process is not useful if the rest of the processes continue to take the time that they do. Hence, understanding what adds value or not to a *customer's life* level is critical.

The second aspect of *redefining market spaces* requires pushing the envelope of existing businesses (Coke thinking of shares of stomach, diamond jewellers thinking of share of money spent on luxury indulgences, an Indian hair colour company thinking of share of black hair in the world, etc.); or creating new never-before product markets; or proactively driving segmentation in the market along different variables than the ones that currently exist.

A leading FMCG company was not getting enough quality applications at business schools because it was not in the preferred product segments of investment banks or consulting companies. Nor was it in the preferred job segments of foreign posting or lots of money. It decided to redefine the market space by driving segmentation of a different kind: CEO type (who runs a real business and has control over its shape and destiny) and consultant type (who gives advice, but actually does not have any control or depth in shaping a business). It decided not to compete for the investment bank preferers, but to fight for the consulting company applicants by driving a wedge (segmentation) and detaching a piece of territory (a segment) that the company could dominate. The insight for this did *not* come from conventional market research approaches of asking students who were graduating what their criteria were, in order of preference, when choosing a job. It came from asking: 'How come young people have such herd mentality? Why is no one willing to march to the beat of a different drummer?' It came from hearing people two and three years into their workplaces saying they were frustrated with a consulting career or an operating line job for a set of reasons which were to do with the very core of their nature and mental makeup and what they enjoyed doing. It came from asking: 'How come on Ivy League American campuses, where this

Figure 8.3: Staging a Revolution: Changing the Rules and Leaving Others Behind

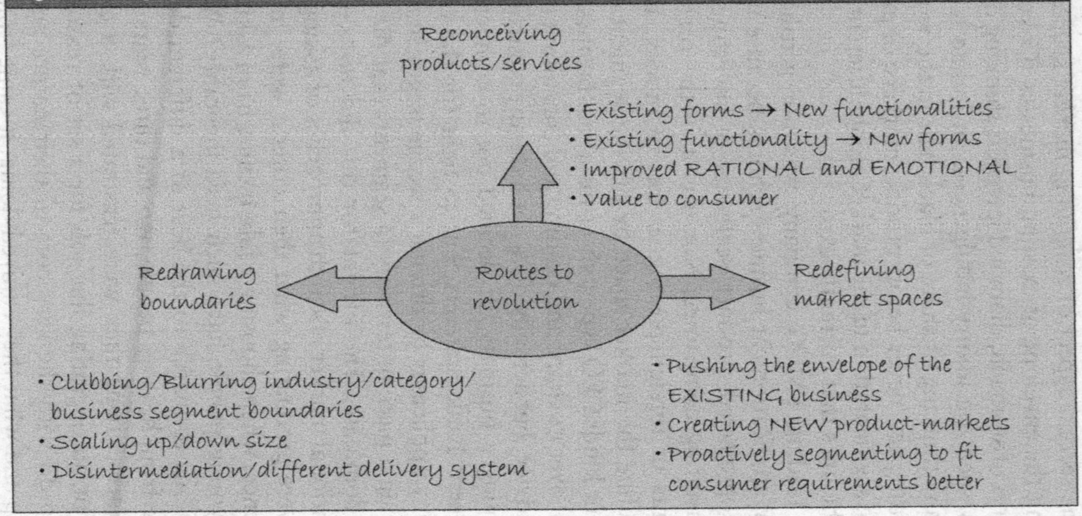

Reconceiving products/services
- Existing forms → New functionalities
- Existing functionality → New forms
- improved RATIONAL and EMOTIONAL value to consumer

Routes to revolution

Redefining market spaces
- Pushing the envelope of the EXISTING business
- creating NEW product-markets
- Proactively segmenting to fit consumer requirements better

Redrawing boundaries
- Clubbing/Blurring industry/category/business segment boundaries
- Scaling up/down size
- Disintermediation/different delivery system

Source: Adapted from Hamel (1996).

pattern is repeated, a handful of 'regular' companies still hold on to their supremacy?' The answer was that it is possible to came out a segment of students with self-images of being the 'CEO type' (as opposed to being a 'consultant type'), and to become the company of choice for them.

The job of functional marketing then was to decide how this strategy could be implemented. In order to drive segmentation they used their understanding of the psyche and behaviour of these young people and devised a plan that involved connecting student coordinators with an aptitude testing firm of repute, and offering to pay for their service as requested by students. As a result of this testing, animated discussions happened in the dining rooms and coffee shops—on whether you were a 'consultant type', or a 'CEO type' thus driving the desired segmentation among students.

The third aspect of creating industry revolution through *redrawing of boundaries* is about blurring industry/ category divides (edutainment, nutraceuticals, iPad, etc.) through scaling up or down businesses or designing radically different delivery systems. Again, this comes from innovations that are relevant to consumers, convergence and do not add complexity, but create simplicity and often from very different pricing and delivery models—*pay as you use* and *service not product on tap* being the two that work very well in India.

Sometimes, attempts to create an industry revolution fall flat when consumer insight is weak. We once worked for an Indian tractor company that noticed that the market for custom hiring of tractors by farmers was growing. They decided that rather than fighting for a share of the purchased tractor market, they would play in the custom hiring market. This play ended in disaster despite a whole lot of market research amongst farmers already hiring tractors on how often/what kind/what price/what service they wanted. As long as they asked their customers why they were hiring and not buying, the answers were predictable and not very helpful. Had they stopped for a minute to fully understand the dynamics of the custom hiring market, they would not have rushed in with such logic. The story of the market was that the farmers were increasingly having to buy larger HP tractors than their purse and their farm economics permitted (since most Indian farmers have small farms). The reason for doing so was because small tractors, which were affordable, were not performing as they were required to. Marketers also decided that the market 'is shifting to larger HP' and did not make any effort to fix the small-tractor performance problem. As a result of having to buy unaffordable larger tractors, farmers who bought them were renting them out to earn enough extra money to pay their monthly instalments of the bank loan. Therefore, for every new tractor sold, there was a custom hiring capacity already being created, and the buyers' economic logic driving pricing was quite different (better) than that of the company!

In Table 8.1, we provide a broad set of consumer information and insight areas that will aid strategists in applying Hamel's framework for creating industry revolution and gaining competitive advantage (refer to Figure 8.2).

Mindset: Acknowledging the obvious and acting on it

More often than not, there are opportunities that are obvious and available for creating customer perceived value advantage; yet businesses prefer not to pursue them, either because they are difficult to implement or because they are so obvious that they are easy to miss! Paint companies in India often spend millions of rupees trying to obtain

---

Box 8.1: Consumer Information Inputs for Applying Hamel's Framework

Holistic market structure maps of a need arena

- Define need arena (transportation or security for household or safety of children).
- Profile who all exist with this need with what level of intensity and why.
- Map all methods of fulfilling these needs including 'none-do nothing'.
- Map quantitatively who is using what, when, how. Do not start with what is being used by whom. Start with customer pool or base.
- Examine multiple usages, reasons for non-usage, contexts for multiple usage, etc.

Understanding usage behaviour and levels of satisfaction

- How, why, context of use.
- Map all points of the end-to-end experience not just the parts that you play in (airlines often do not look at challenges customers face from door to door or paint companies in the customers' process of acquiring a painted wall. Hence they miss out on how they can re-conceive products or services or redraw boundaries or redefine market spaces and significantly disrupt existing industries).
- Understand customer value processing (he who understands it best can create disproportionate 'value to customer-cost to company' equations and win from it).
- Understand relationship—between need arena and fulfilment methods (for example, why do people have both two-wheelers and cars? What do they use each for? Therefore, is there a 'car-mate' two-wheeler with features which will be different? Is there a case for dual case and scooter dealerships rather than individual specialized ones?).

199

consumer insight that will help them grow their business by getting more consumers to paint more often or to create value advantage for their brands in what they believe is an undifferentiated market. We often urge paint companies to notice the obvious: that they sell paint while the customer buys a painted wall—and that nobody is 'in charge' in between. The painters blame the paint for bad results, the paint company the painter. In India, painting a house is an excruciating process. If paint companies could offer a decent painting service—speedy, well done and with a crew that is safe and reliable, then most of us would paint our houses more often.

Yet, despite the obvious power of that rivalry proposition, most paint companies do not venture into setting up painting services. Instead, they prefer to conclude that painting is a 'low involvement' activity (For whom? Certainly not the person who has to live with the painted walls for several years and who cringes when guests come and notice shabby walls). They, thus, proceed to build rivalry propositions around getting the exact colour that one has in mind and, hence, putting up very expensive colour machines in retail outlets, modernizing the dirty traditional paint outlets housing these machines in order to tempt customers to use the facility and then being surprised that other companies are following suit and obliterating the competitive advantage.

Actually, customers do want to experiment with colours and express themselves through colours but as with any colour-oriented business, be it home furnishing or personal accessories, there is a worry about not knowing how to, and about the consequences of getting it wrong. But they want a proposition that includes not just a range of colours and the facility to pick their dream colour, but also someone that helps them in being able to use colour effectively and in a de-risked way (Who wants to live with wall colour disasters and mistakes until the next round of painting?). They want guidance to help them use colours to optically enlarge or brighten or dull down rooms, as the need may be, or to draw attention to expensive paintings, or to be able to mix and match colours in exotic but harmonious ways. This is, indeed, a very valuable consumer perceived value advantage to build upon for a paint business as a whole. However, paint companies pick up the consumer signals of 'it's all about colours' and think of it as a way to expand their range of colours even further. They do not pick up on the rest of the opportunity. Perhaps part of the reason is the difficulty in delivering on propositions managing a high-quality painter force or offering customized advice on colour in a cost-effective way that really result in superior consumer perceived value.

Mindset: Questioning conventional wisdom

Asking the magical questions: why not and how come

In order to drive better consumer insight for being able to 'think what no one else has thought about that which everyone sees', ask the magic questions: *Why not* and *how come*? How come scooter sales are declining and motorcycle sales growing though (a) it is hard to transport an entire family on a motorcycle and (b) the average Indian family size has not declined, nor has the 'family outing' institution disappeared? How come with so many nuclear families no one talks about the market of the old parents living alone? How come in India we have no readymade *chapatis* available of acceptable quality, though women hate making *chapatti*s and we eat 1 trillion a year? How come if farm sizes have not increased, tractor sales of bigger tractors are increasing? Why has the bed and bath category stayed frozen in time even though every other aspect of home décor has moved on? Why is it that young people using Category X are content to buy their father's brands instead of rejecting it? And so on.

In several cases, the answer will emerge that it is supply-side forces and not consumer preferences that have created the existing scenarios, and, hence, there is opportunity for a genuinely customer-based strategy to create huge strategic differentiation and competitive advantage (via consumer advantage).

Re-examining the 'holy cows'

We often ask companies we consult with to make a list of the 'doesn't everybody know' assumptions about consumers that drive their strategy and apply the 'how come' test to them. For instance, one could ask: 'How come the rural consumer market is "not-yet-ready" for hair dyes?' Is it because rural men and women have no need for looking younger than they are? Or is it because they do not like chemicals? The subsequent questions would be: 'How come herbal hair dye does not sell?' or 'How come they use Y and Z products on their body which are chemical?' One could similarly ask:

> 'How come the bottled water market is exploding but penetration of water filters is so low? How come in a country which has such a history, culture and tradition of using fragrance-giving products, perfumes do not sell?'

202

The point we want to forcefully make is that many of these assumptions that drive strategy can and must be validated by talking to customers. We often wonder why seven people sitting in a dark boardroom discuss and debate answers to these questions in a vacuum—Why second guess the consumer? Why not ask him/her?

Approach: Creating new markets

The *how come* or the *why not* questions often lead to opening up of huge new markets for growth. We were at a nutraceuticals company that supplies organic products like lycopene, lutein, spirulina and omega 3 to health food, pharmaceutical and cosmeceutical industries. The global markets for these are well established, but in India the markets are non-existent. The company strategy, therefore, was built around global markets and did not anticipate playing in the domestic Indian market. The first question to ask when developing customer-based business strategy for this business would be: How come we have no market for these products in India; although, when we look around, we see several signs of sophisticated activity in these end-user industries (enumerate the signs and look at them together)? When will the market 'mature' given the rate of growth in income and sophistication of a billion people, 250–300 million of whom are high-end consumers?

Putting the two together, analysis will show that the market is ready to be created, and suppliers of these intermediate products are the ones lagging behind because they do not differentiate between market creation in ready markets (painless, quick) and market creation in not ready markets (painful, expensive, may not succeed).

Approach: Shaping current markets

A related issue is that of shaping current markets and evolving them to a higher performance point. We are often told by companies that they want to be shapers of markets and not adapters to existing rules of the game. They say that this strategic posture of shaping will get them the competitive and strategic advantage they need. Yet the question that always separates the interiors from the action is 'How do we know the market is ready for shaping?' If we were to elaborate this question as 'How do we know people or customers or consumers are ready to change their behaviour and adopt something different?' then it does not seem to be a difficult and daunting one to answer. We often ask clients to listen to what customers are saying and ask. 'What do I need to hear in order to believe that the market is ready for shaping?' Sometimes the signals that the consumer is ready for change can come from extreme defensiveness in tone when they talk of what they currently do; sometimes it can be the leap of curiosity and excitement when you show them something better that is available elsewhere; sometimes the answer may lie not in their stated happiness or unhappiness but with the huge effort they are putting into achieving the results that they want with the current options they are using. In all cases, we are making the point that even apparently large and tough questions can be answered quite simply and logically by talking to customers, if you see the problem of forecasting market shifts into one of seeing what changes in customer behaviour are required in order to shift the market.

Approach: Reading and riding future macro trends

In order to predict the future, as we have said, one has to be able to see what no one else has seen, or bothered to notice, and think what no one else has thought about that which everyone sees. One way to approach this is to create competitive advantage by reading and riding macro trends early.

Several strategy development exercises do point to macro trends. However, the effort is often restricted to trying to understand the implications of each trend in a direct, first-degree effect kind of way. This leads to not very insightful conclusions and does not reveal opportunities to fundamentally reshape businesses. For example, we in India are all aware of the rise in the number of women working outside the home, of their increasing educational qualification and confidence. However, a real insight based on this trend would require two kinds of investigation of consumers. One, what really is the resultant change in a woman's behaviour with respect to her home and the outside world? It may reveal that even as she does more new things outside the home, she maintains a balance in her ecosystem by doing more of the old things at home. This could point to a whole set of new products and propositions to help her achieve and maintain this delicate balance, and companies could decide which 'her' they want to target. Second, it requires a lot of investigation to understand exactly how her home management is changing. What are her attitudes to the inventory of household products of all kinds? Has her buying behaviour changed? Have her entertaining habits changed? How does her time allocation work? How has her mindset with respect to her role changed? How does all this impact refrigerators, kitchen durables, retailing, men's products environment, children, etc.?

Another example: as capitation fees in medical colleges increase, and as other options available for higher education increase, are the type of people going to medical school changing? Will they be far more business and commerce oriented than the generation of doctors before them? What are the resultant implications for a pharmaceutical or health care company? Or, what kind of pressures will doctors be facing as patients increasingly get information from the web? As the balance of knowledge shifts more towards the patient, what does it do to a doctor's business and to his behaviour as a response? What could this mean to a pharmaceutical company in terms of how to compete? As the Indian workforce gets more and more self-employed, what does it mean for a health care company? Add to this the rise of health insurance and the fact that middle-income people are more careful about their health than rich people (hospital expenses, need to work, lack of access to better doctors and hospitals). What opportunities for building customer perceived value advantage offers are up for a pharmaceutical company?

Similar questions have to be asked in B2B companies as well: A polyurethane company we worked for identified three verticals as important: use in panels for making office partitions, refrigerators, and cars. In the latter two categories, at the time of our study, capacities were excess and refrigerator and car companies were determined to hold on to product quality (in light of cut-throat competition) at the lowest price. How does one play in such a market and compete to win? Perhaps value can be added through innovative services.

In the office panels' end-use segment, they missed a critical force that was providing an opportunity to shape the segment: business organization structures were getting flatter and less hierarchical, and with that, the offices were moving more and more to the open office plan. People were doing even more work over the telephone. The result? The need for sound-proof panels for open offices and the service for designing open offices better on this count was very high. Suddenly, the ability to offer functional benefit and create consumer perceived value advantage become available. Again, as in the case of paints, the *where* and *how to compete* had to include the augmented product of designing offices as well as improving soundproofing. What do organization structures have to do with the polyurethane business? As B2B suppliers of raw material, it is imperative for companies to keep track of what is happening in their customers' industries and individual businesses in order to spot future opportunities and trends. Yet, far too often, B2B companies gather consumer insight by talking to their customer about their own company's business, and not about the customer's business. They thus miss out on valuable opportunities for value creation and competitive advantage creation. One of the exercises we make our B2B clients do is to have conversations with their customers about customer concerns, worries, business plans relating to customer's business *without* mentioning their own products even once.

Approach: Read the change web

C.K. Prahalad makes the point that reading change signals individually runs the danger of strategists dismissing each signal as being too small and too weak to be of much consequence. However, when several small changes come together, they send out a loud and clear message that there is a powerful change wave about to happen. Therefore, reading and riding macro trends and changes in the consumer or customer world requires that all changes be read together. We call it seeing the *change web*. Such a way of seeing helps detect imminent value shifts that throw up opportunities for creating serious consumer advantage ahead of competition. The way to identify a change web is to look at all connected aspects driving needs and ask, 'So what?' Figure 8.3 gives an example of the change web in health care in India.

On the one hand, there is more money available to patients, thanks to health insurance and life insurance premiums being linked to how fit you are to begin with! On the other hand, the 'power distance' between doctor and patient is decreasing thanks to information on the web—the doctor is transitioning from being 'God' to being a service provider. Add to this the fact that doctors are looking for a return on investment on their expensive education, and there is no question that the business of being a doctor is changing. How are they coping? What dimensions are they looking for help on? What are the new opportunities and new ways to engage them that pharmaceutical companies need to think about?

Similarly, drivers of changing needs from a five-star hotel include a whole host of small changes from the fact that CEOs are getting younger, so the fact that remote working is now accepted, and your hotel room is an acceptable place to work from; that availability of flights are on the increase, and staying the night in another town is not a compulsion. Entertainment patterns are changing too, as are lifestyle patterns; flatter organization structures and less-hierarchical behaviour are evident. All of then taken together could point to the opportunity for a totally different kind of hospitality business—the hotels of the future.

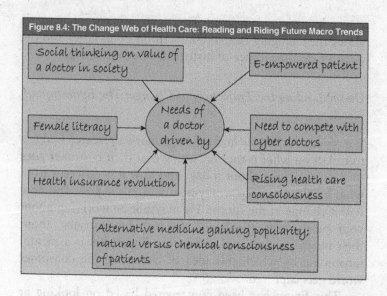

Figure 8.4: The Change Web of Health Care: Reading and Riding Future Macro Trends

A client in the home-cleaning business in the UK spotted an imminent shift in what customers would value by looking at the intersection of what was happening in two areas: the kinds of homes (used where) and the types of women (who uses). He concluded that homes in England were beginning to look less like fortresses and becoming more open, with patios, open conservatories, etc. This eco-friendly movement, which did not see openness as contact with bad germs, was happening at the same time as feminism gaining ground in the mainstream, making women less obsessed with the tasks of cooking and cleaning being done to perfection. The answer to the classical strategy question for the CEO 'What kind of future do you need to prepare your business for?' was quite clear. As any CEO will tell you, the first moment of panic after recognizing such a shift is: 'Oh my God, my R&D is not at all geared for this. We have the wrong research projects pipeline.' The next moment of panic is about the changing face of competition boundaries and the possible disappearance of historical value advantage.

Understanding the Trajectory of Change: The Evolution of Needs

We often ask clients who have large market research budgets to reflect on what is that one thing that their customer goes to sleep worrying about today, and how it is different from what he went to sleep worrying about in the past, and how will it change in the future. He may not be worrying about your business at all—he or she may be worrying about their business, their life, and so on. Figure 8.4 is a mental mnemonic by which this idea of change in the consumer world gets captured.

This figure has been constructed based on looking at what is being written and spoken in the ecosystem, and based on conversations with customers or consumers about *their* world. There are themes that consumers thought about yesterday (residual), there are themes that they think about today (dominant) and there are themes that they will think about tomorrow (emergent). How does one understand *emergent themes* in consumers' minds and business or lives that are relevant to a strategist's business? Typically, every customer/consumer/universe has a set of innovators who break compromises ahead of the others or a set of early adopters of new ways of doing things, or cutting-edge desperates who feel the need before others do and invent their own solutions for it. For example, small and medium Indian enterprises manufacturers for large brands in the US are likely to be early responders to demands for corporate social responsibility and environment-friendly sustainable

210

manufacturing. What such customers want from you today could set the tone for what others will want tomorrow. Lower-income, educated working women might innovate solutions today for how they run their households with time-saving amenities and practices designed for their low budgets, which may be the way the rest of the market will evolve in the future. This group would be the early adopters because they have low income, but higher order needs and have to find ways of coping.

The research needed to understand what emergent trends are, is actually quite simple—listening to leading edge or progressive customers. As we have already discussed, the questions must range around the change in *their* lives and mindsets and concerns and how it impacts the *need arena* under discussion. The questions should not range around how the supplier and product world is changing. Figure 8.5 shows findings from a set of focus groups for a consumer nutrition and health business.

Housewives and mothers used rich analogies to explain to us how the world of health and nutrition was changing.

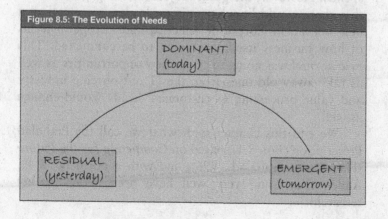

Figure 8.5: The Evolution of Needs

DOMINANT (today)

RESIDUAL (yesterday)

EMERGENT (tomorrow)

They likened it to changes in tuition teachers and doctors. Earlier, tuition teachers came to tutor academically weak children. But nowadays they tutor high-achieving children. Earlier, doctors were general practitioners. But nowadays they are specialists. However, there is an emergent trend of a new kind of general practitioner who is holistically taking charge of a family's health.

It is important to remember that the only way to know what your customers go to sleep worrying about is to talk to them about their business and their lives, not about *your* business. Yet, most market research tends to be around asking customers how they relate to your product/service world rather than understanding how the worlds can be connected. After the meltdown of 2008 in global financial markets, and the distress in businesses around the world, India's software industry mostly kept asking customers the question: 'What will you do to your IT budgets?' They made the connection between companies who had received bailouts from the government and their changed decision-making behaviour as a result with respect to IT spends. However, the point they did not engage with was that there would be what opinion leaders were calling a *new normal* in Corporate America and Europe in terms of how business itself was going to be conducted. This *new normal* was going to create new opportunities as well as take away old ones from the IT outsourcing industry and value processing in customers' heads would change as well.

We end this chapter with what we call the Prahalad Prescription (Box 8.1), based on *Competing for the Future* (Hamel and Prahalad 1996), and with a poem by W.H. Auden that could very well have been about market research!

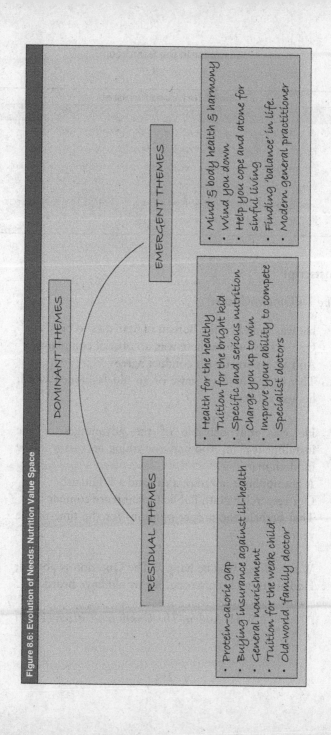

Figure 8.6: Evolution of Needs: Nutrition Value Space

DOMINANT THEMES

RESIDUAL THEMES

EMERGENT THEMES

- Protein-calorie gap
- Buying insurance against ill-health
- General nourishment
- Tuition for the weak child
- Old-world 'family doctor'

- Health for the healthy
- Tuition for the bright kid
- Specific and serious nutrition
- Charge you up to win
- Improve your ability to compete
- Specialist doctors

- Mind & body health & harmony
- Wind you down
- Help you cope and atone for sinful living
- Finding 'balance' in life.
- Modern general practitioner

Box 8.2: The Prahalad Prescription

- Avoid the tyranny of the served product-market.
- Be eclectic—look through multiple lenses.
- Empathize with human needs (customers are people, not merely buyers of your products).
- Understand the change web of drivers of change to get value foresight (read the future).

Postscript

The Unknown Citizen

He was found by the Bureau of Statistics to be
One against whom there was no official complaint,
And all reports on his conduct agree
That in the modern sense of an old fashioned word,
he was a saint

He was fully sensible of the advantages of the
installment plan, And had everything necessary to the
modern man
A gramophone, a radio, a car and a Frigidaire
Our researchers into Public Opinion are content
That he held the proper opinions for the time of the
year

Was he free? Was he happy? The Question is absurd;
Had anything been wrong, we would have heard.

—W.H. Auden, *The Unknown Citizen* (1939)

CHAPTER 9

Foundation or Baseline Analyses for Strategy Development

All strategy frameworks and processes suggest that the foundation or baseline analyses for strategy development comprise: (a) an analysis of the external world in order to identify opportunities and threats that could affect the business and (b) an internal analysis of the company in order to identify its strengths and weaknesses. These two analyses, when read together, will provide the guidelines for enumerating and then choosing the strategic paths to take in order to achieve the business goals. We have mentioned these analyses in passing in Chapter 2 because we believe that several other strategy books have dealt with these traditional analyses in great depth. In this chapter we have focused on a set of additional and very specific analyses based on a deep dive into the customer world, since we felt that such customer-based analyses are traditionally not done by business strategists.

We do believe, without question, that doing the traditional baseline analyses at the beginning of the strategy development exercise is extremely useful. It is a disciplined way in which to marshal all the facts and the key stories in

215

Figure 9.1: The CBBS Framework: Strengthening Strategy Foundation Analyses

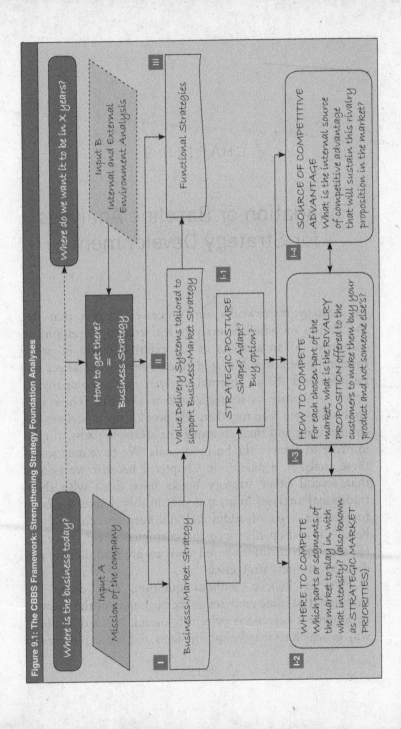

all parts of the ecosystem in which the business operates. More importantly, it also forces reflection on how the future may be different from the past, and forces development of 'future-proof' business strategy. In this chapter, while we do not go into the 101 'how to' discussions, we do provide templates of how such baseline or foundational analyses that traditionally form the basic toolkit for the strategy developer can be conducted and interpreted through the *customer-based* lens, so that they contribute more forcefully to the customer-based element of business strategy. We see these foundational analyses as being meant to collectively provide a broad map of the entire terrain in which strategic paths could potentially lie. Such a map should clearly highlight where the minefields lie (for example, shrinking customer segment or needs becoming obsolete) and the oases are growth segments or specialized customer needs or competition-disadvantaged islands; it should specify the heights of the mountain ranges to be climbed (for example, distribution system wields a great deal of buyer power for the following reasons), and the depths and the widths of the rivers to be crossed (brand loyalty is very high in such markets and the brand leader is strongly entrenched); it should mark the fertile areas where seeds of change sown will easily bear fruit (lifestyle changes in households due to working women), and the barren areas where returns on effort are (for example, no decline in availability of grey market assembled kits with superb service back up); it should highlight where different consumer 'tribes' live, and who they are; and so on. This broad-brush map must also serve to point out changes that are already afoot or likely to occur in the next three to five years, and take a stab at how the future could directionally unfold in the next ten years. As we have discussed in earlier chapters, this map should not only provide direction on strategy to achieve goals, but also be useful to define the goals themselves.

In this chapter, we will:

- Briefly describe the building blocks that such foundational analyses comprise.
- Show how to connect these analyses with the world of customers; hence, enabling them to add value to customer-based business strategy.
- Provide some pointers from experience with such analyses on how to sharpen them.

BUILDING BLOCKS OF BASELINE OR FOUNDATIONAL ANALYSIS

We think of the external and internal analyses required for business strategy development as being made up of five building blocks:

1. Customer view.
2. Market or industry (supply and supply-chain view of the world).
3. External environment (technology, regulation, geopolitical issues, etc., which envelope the context in which the industry and the firm exists).
4. Competitor view.
5. Self or company-internal view.

Briefly described ahead is what the contents of each module could contain, and the customer-based questions which the analyses should answer.

Building Block 1: Customer Analysis

The key question that this analysis must answer is: 'What is going on in the world of the customers that presents opportunities to exploit and threats that need to be de-risked?'

The systematic way to arrive at answers for this question would be to examine the customer world from different aspects, as outlined in the Figure 9.1.

To begin with, this analysis must be done for the current scenario. In addition, in order to improve the strategist's understanding, a documentation of the changes that have occurred in the past five years would also be very useful.

After the current scenario mapping, it is time to attempt to see how the future will unfold.

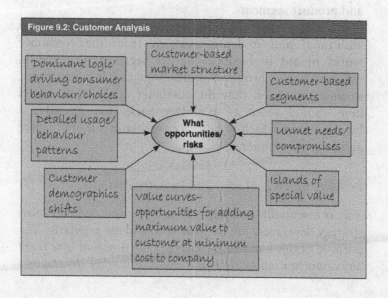

Figure 9.2: Customer Analysis

'Dominant logic' driving consumer behaviour/choices

Customer-based market structure

Customer-based segments

Detailed usage/behaviour patterns

What opportunities/risks

Unmet needs/compromises

Customer demographics shifts

Value curves-opportunities for adding maximum value to customer at minimum cost to company

Islands of special value

Given ahead is a suggested systematic process of analysis that could help to develop a clearer point of view of how the future will unfold:

- Current scenario map
- Changes from the past
- Listing of drivers of change in the foreseeable future, with gradation of importance and impact
- Impact of drivers in each box
- Changes in the map as a result of all likely changes

The key point to note here is that this analysis is about factors intrinsic to consumers—the term 'product' or 'product category' does not figure here. We find that companies have a great deal of difficulty doing this and tend to immediately slip into the comfort zone of product and product segments.

In the earlier chapters, we have suggested several additional and in-depth analyses from the consumer world to aid in business-market segmentation and in value or rivalry proposition development. It is important to note, however, that the customer analyses discussed here should serve as a starter pack that provides a baseline from which to advance further in a more literate and focused manner.

Building Block 2: Market and Industry Analysis

This is essentially a supply-side analysis and one that most strategy developers are familiar with and use regularly. The purpose of this analysis is to answer the question *'Are there any opportunities or risks as a result of market structure or "rules of the game" tacit agreements among suppliers, or as a result of likely changes in these?'*

We often point out to our clients that customer behaviour is shaped not just by customer-intrinsic variables, but also by supply-side factors. Hence, the elements of this block of analysis should completely capture what is going on in the market that strategy developers need to know about. Most companies stop at the level of such supply-side analysis. We, however, urge our clients to push this analysis all the way to 'So what does it mean for the customer world? Will it result in changes in what people buy or how they make their choices or their value processing?' (See Figure 9.2.)

As should be the case for all modules, the focus of market or industry analysis should be on understanding what the current situation is, what has changed in the market or industry from the past and on how the future will be different and why. (Note: For this analysis, we use the word 'market' as it is traditionally conceptualized as being the sum total of sales of all suppliers and all product types in a given product space.)

Building Block 3: External Environment Analysis

The question that this module should answer is: *'Are there any discontinuities that are likely to happen or any changes that could hit the business negatively or provide opportunities for exploitation?'* (See Figure 9.3.)

As discussed in the earlier section, companies usually do this analysis in great detail, but do not drive it to the level where it can answer the corollary question, 'So what is the implication on consumer behaviour or market structure as a result of these changes and why?' For example, it was a

221

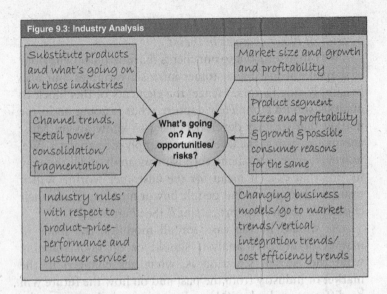

Figure 9.3: Industry Analysis

Substitute products and what's going on in those industries

Market size and growth and profitability

Channel trends, Retail power consolidation/ fragmentation

What's going on? Any opportunities/ risks?

Product segment sizes and profitability & growth & possible consumer reasons for the same

Industry 'rules' with respect to product–price–performance and customer service

Changing business models/go to market trends/vertical integration trends/ cost efficiency trends

shift in the physical infrastructure building activity from the developed world to the developing world in the 1970s that gave Komatsu an opportunity to win over Caterpillar because they understood that one of the implications of this shift was a big change in consumer behaviour— the behaviour of developing market governments as customers was quite different from that of developed markets customers, which required new value packages and new business systems to deliver them, including renting rather than selling equipment. Another example is how a change in regulation banning overloading of trucks in northern India could imply a change in the value consumers attach to the strength of their load-bearing front tyres, and could render valueless, company business strategies based on the traditional value-spaces-based segment of extra load-enabling front tyres, normal load-bearing tyres and speed enabling tyres.

Building Block 4: Competition Analysis

The method of competition analysis has been well documented and described in several books, starting with Michael Porter's *Competitive Strategy* (1980) and *Cases in Competitive Strategy* (1982). We suggest that the key question to ask when analysing competition is: '*What do they have that we do not, that could kill us in the market?*' Merely understanding that competitors have lower costs or a more disciplined distributor–retailer coverage system or a certain cash flow is not enough. The question to ask is: 'What does it limit or enable them to do to create customer perceived value advantage?'

We also believe that competitor analysis must focus as much on the insides of competitor companies and more on their conduct towards customers and other players in the market. What is the dominant logic that drives the customer-related actions of a company? Is it 'market share at all costs, squeeze out competition'? Or is it no investing

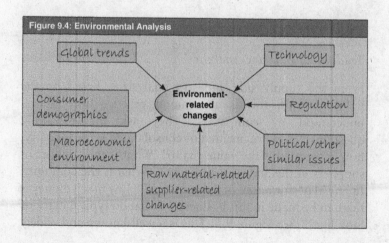

Figure 9.4: Environmental Analysis

ahead in consumers or markets without profits? Is Economic Value Added (EVA) the king? Cash is king? Valuation is the key? We also suggest a measurement of the customers' view of the competition to fully understand one's competitors (Figure 9.4).

As in the other analyses, a map of the present, the changes from the past, an identification of what factors could drive change, and an actual modelling of what changes are likely to occur in each future scenario are necessary to develop a fool-proof, futuristic strategy.

Building Block 5: Self-Analysis of Company

The key questions that this kind of analysis should answer is: *'What is the company's ability to compete in the market? What does it have which will help it create customer-perceived value advantage?* How ready is it to exploit opportunities or how de-risked is it from changes in the world outside?' (See Figure 9.5)

TWO KEY SUMMARY ANALYSES

Traditional Industry Analysis

From the supply side, industry analysis is based on the industry itself; this is a common practice and is well understood by companies. They ask the following questions: 'How fragmented or consolidated is the industry, how integrated is the value chain?' 'What is the conduct of suppliers in this industry and why?' 'What is the combined financial performance of the industry?' 'How much money is there to be made in this business?' 'What do typical margins look like?' (See Figure 9.7) This is a well-known and widely

224

Foundation or Baseline Analyses for Strategy Development

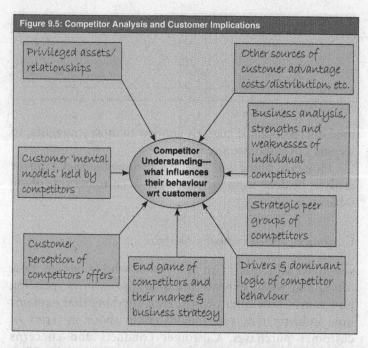

Figure 9.5: Competitor Analysis and Customer Implications

- Privileged assets/relationships
- Other sources of customer advantage costs/distribution, etc.
- Business analysis, strengths and weaknesses of individual competitors
- Customer 'mental models' held by competitors
- Competitor Understanding—what influences their behaviour wrt customers
- Strategic peer groups of competitors
- Customer perception of competitors' offers
- End game of competitors and their market & business strategy
- Drivers & dominant logic of competitor behaviour

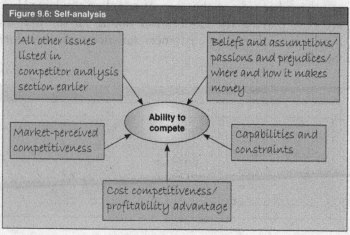

Figure 9.6: Self-analysis

- All other issues listed in competitor analysis section earlier
- Beliefs and assumptions/passions and prejudices/where and how it makes money
- Market-perceived competitiveness
- Ability to compete
- Capabilities and constraints
- Cost competitiveness/profitability advantage

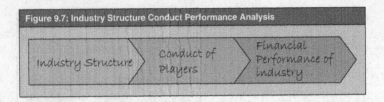

Figure 9.7: Industry Structure Conduct Performance Analysis

Industry Structure ⟩ Conduct of Players ⟩ Financial Performance of industry ⟩

used microeconomic analysis familiar to most strategists, so we will not elaborate any further.

However, along with this, we also suggest that a mirror analysis be done from the consumer or customer side of the table.

Customer-centred Industry Analysis

Customer structure in an analysis of who is buying, how often, and what; expenditure analysis—who is spending how much, how often, when, etc., anything that explains how industry size and growth come about in terms of customer purchases. Customer conducts and concerns are the other side of the coin of supplier conduct. How are *they* playing the game? And taking all the options available to them, are customers satisfied with their lot? (See Figure 9.8.)

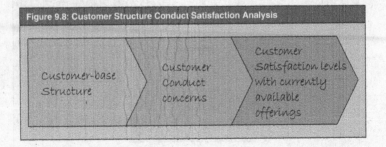

Figure 9.8: Customer Structure Conduct Satisfaction Analysis

Customer-base Structure ⟩ Customer Conduct concerns ⟩ Customer Satisfaction levels with currently available offerings ⟩

Box 9.1: SCS Analysis

STRUCTURE

Are there a lot of people buying a little bit of the product once in a while, or is it a few heavy users who form the core and account for 70 per cent of the revenue, the remaining 30 per cent being transient to the category? Are multiple categories used or just one to fulfil their need?

CONDUCT AND CONCERNS

What is the customer conduct and concerns with respect to the category? Bargain hunting or value maximizing? Is the focus on productivity or price? Do they replace often and upgrade? Are they brand loyal?

SATISFACTION

Are they satisfied? Satisfaction here refers to the overall level of satisfaction with the industry as a whole.

GENERAL HELPFUL TIPS FOR CONDUCTING BASELINE ANALYSIS

- Keep analysis fact based (all the data needed is in here).
- For each building block, develop a *story line*, that is, what are the three key stories that this analysis is telling?
- Put all the story lines across all building blocks together and see what they are saying.
- For each building block, assess the current situation, how this has changed from the past and what is likely in the future.
- Put all *future views* together across all building blocks and ask: 'How do we see the future unfold?'
- Most important of all, every piece of analysis, whether an individual element or a collective story, must be pushed to the level of 'so what does it mean at the level

of customers or consumers? How will it change market
structure or customer behaviour?'

As we said earlier in this chapter, we find that this set of
analytic building blocks forms the baseline from which
further and more focused analysis needs to be done when
developing strategy. This is the backdrop, the map of the
world in which the strategy must reside. Put another way,
we say this analysis is like a detailed map of the terrain—
it points to minefields and fertile grounds and charts
the path and progress of other travellers in this terrain;
environmental analysis is somewhat like a seismic map or a
weather forecast.

Since it has multiple and different uses at various stages
of the strategy development process, we suggest that this
entire analytic module be done right at the beginning of
the strategy development exercise to provide guidelines and
navigation principles for finding the strategic answers, both
in terms of narrowing the field of play and in terms of fine-
tuning further analysis.

Putting Customer-Based Business Strategy into Practice in Organizations

RESOLVING THE TYRANNY OF 'OR'

We are often told by practicing managers that they totally agree with our CBBS approach, *but* . . . And there is always the 'yes, but'. All the arguments and concerns that they raise have merit; so we thought we must end this book with a discussion on some of them. Most of the arguments principally centre on what C.K. Prahalad called 'the tyranny of OR'. Should a company pursue an 'outside-in' strategy, chase after new opportunities, and run the risk of not having enough capability to deliver? OR should it be pragmatic and prudent and 'inside-out', aiming only for those market opportunities which it already has the capabilities to deliver? Should it be leading the customer OR should it be customer-led? Should it pursue profitability, OR should it pursue customer delight, given that one usually comes at the expense of the other?

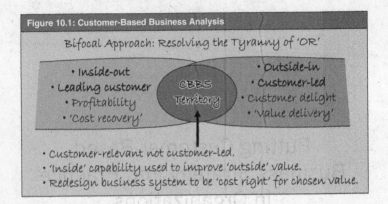

Figure 10.1: Customer-Based Business Analysis

Bifocal Approach: Resolving the Tyranny of 'OR'

- Inside-out
- Leading customer
- Profitability
- 'Cost recovery'

CBBS Territory

- Outside-in
- Customer-led
- Customer delight
- 'Value delivery'

- Customer-relevant not customer-led.
- 'Inside' capability used to improve 'outside' value.
- Redesign business system to be 'cost right' for chosen value.

BIFOCAL VISION

To help practicing managers deal with 'the tyranny of OR' we offer the concept of bifocal vision, which is best illustrated in Figure 10.1.

Bifocal vision requires that outside opportunities be weighed against inside capabilities—and capability to acquire and build new capabilities is a big capability too—and the common space between the two is the territory we are suggesting that strategy focuses on.

We want to emphatically state that the CBBS way is not about finding *new* lines of business. It is about strategizing your current business better. It is an outside-in way to think about what you need to do to win in your *current* line of business, by defining your current line of business through the eyes and minds of customers rather than through the lens of products and technologies and competition and other such supply-sided views.

There is no tyranny of OR either, in the 'Should I be customer led or should I lead the customer?' To our mind, there is no conflict at all between the two. Of course, businesses should lead the customer because they know more about what is possible. As we have said earlier, it is the job of customers to have problems and the job of businesses to resolve them. We certainly hope businesses will go beyond what customers can dream of. However, our caution continuously has been that the actions the company undertakes in the name of the customer, on behalf of the customer and for the customer, must be *relevant* to the customer and in line with the way the customer's mind and behaviour work.

We have also discussed how to look at the outside world of customer-based opportunity through the lens of the advantages and capabilities that a business has that are unique or special to it—in effect we have advocated, even in our chapter on market segmentation, that companies approach 'outside-in' strategy through the lens of their insides and leverage all their inside capabilities to create outside value.

We have also laid out in detail, in the context of the discussions on 'how to compete', the whole discipline and approach to creating customer-perceived value *and* doing it profitably. We have also discussed the idea that companies need to design innovative value delivery systems and value packages if they need to deliver to a 'challenge cost', which is the maximum amount that the customer is willing to pay. We, therefore, see no 'OR' in customer delight or profitability.

While we are saying that the final solution space for strategy is the overlap between the 'inside-out' end or the 'outside-in' end, we are also saying the first place to start is outside-in. This yields far more strategy breakthroughs because then companies see the outside properly, through the eyes of their customer and in an almost naive manner, and not through the blinkers of their current business. The blinkers and filters can get applied later, but first of all, the seeing of the outside should be comprehensively done.

CONVINCING TOP MANAGEMENT

Whenever we finish conducting an executive development programme with senior managers who are not at the CXO level, but at the level of drafting strategy and certainly influencing it a great deal, the same refrain recurs: 'We agree with you, but how are we going to convince top management to adopt this approach to strategy and the finding of this approach?' Yes, the path of CBBS is a thorny one, but no more thorny than that of any new idea. We teach a wonderful Harvard Business School case study called 'Innovation at 3M' that illustrates the paradigm shifts that CBBS development can cause. A unit of 3M called the Surgical Drapes and Masks business unit makes sterile drapes and masks for infection control during surgery. The market for these had been stagnating for a while and penetration among surgeons in the developed world was quite high, and the business had wanted to generate double-digit growth (in a stagnating market), in a manner that enhanced competitive advantage and provided business to other 3M businesses by leveraging their capabilities in some way. Where and how should they compete to achieve this? After a whole lot of studying the outside world using various innovative methods of study, they came up with three directions that were really no-brainers. One, provide an appropriate offering to surgeons in the developing world so that they can afford to use these products; two, and three, offer two new products to existing users, one being a set of hand-held gadgets that can mop up liquids during surgery and help prevent infection, and the second an anti-microbial product that can be coated on to catheters and other invasive products used during and after surgery. But it was the fourth recommendation that was the problematic one. The team studied the space of 'infection during surgery' holistically rather than restricting themselves to the surgical process alone, given that the mission of the business was to minimize infection in surgery patients. Based on that, it concluded that the business needed to also tackle 'upstream' or 'before surgery' causes for increased risk of infection during surgery, such as malnutrition or diabetes. It should do so by having a set of diagnostic services and processes that could identify individuals with higher levels of infection risk during surgery and have targeted interventions for them before surgery, designed to minimize the risk of infection during surgery. This would fulfil the objectives of driving double-digit growth even in stagnant markets and it would create competitive advantage. The big question was whether it would leverage existing businesses of 3M and, even more fundamentally, whether it should even be considered at all because 'Is this really our business?' The key decision maker was not the kind who appreciated such out of the box (for him, not the consumer!) business thinking, and the case ends with the strategy development team leader about to go in to present her recommendations to him, and wondering whether or not this fourth recommendation should be presented at all! The consumer insight journey had culminated in having to rewriting the existing business strategy—perhaps even rename the business division as 'surgical; infections prevention and control' unit, as it should have been called, to begin with. Clearly, top management has to be prepared to look the tiger in the eye before it tells the troops: 'Go thou and be customer-centric!'

We feel that the best way to get top management 'buy in' into the CBBS way is to have an entire analytics module of the kind discussed in Chapter 9 being presented a day before all strategy retreats of senior management. Even better, if a young team can be made to work on this, then the analysis is even purer. This session should be titled 'outside-in' and has two parts to it: (a) current happenings top management must know about; and (b) longer-term trends: how do we see the future unfold? Every slide must answer the question: 'So what does this mean for market structure and customer behaviour?' The session must end with a sharp discussion by top management on 'Risks and Opportunities for Our Business'. Where there are opportunities identified that are quite different from the organization's present way of doing business, as in the case of 3M, there must be a process of proving the viability of the new business model that needs to be designed.

C.K. Prahalad and Gany Hamel (1996) say that leadership teams in organizations are often unable to sustain even a few hours of discussion about how they see the future, but can go on forever discussing the present, especially if it relates to budgets and targets for the next one year. Similarly, we challenge our client organizations to pool all their assumptions and knowledge about customers and consumers and make a presentation to themselves called 'the customer world of XYZ need arena or value space' and not talk about products even once.

GETTING CUSTOMER-BASED IN DEFINING BUSINESS OBJECTIVES, MISSION AND VISION STATEMENTS AND BRAND IDENTITY TAG LINES

A fundamental gap in customer-centricity in business strategy is the absence of the 'customer' in the mission statement and the absence of all customer-based input into vision and goal setting. We have made the point in earlier chapters that visions, goals or objectives for a business should be specified not just in terms of financials and market share but also in terms of how you want customers to think about you and behave towards you—about what you do for them, how you fit into their lives (how relevant you are to their lives), how distinctive you are as a business, what you do better than your competitors or the other way around, etc.

If we analyse the mission statements and tag lines of corporate brands of most companies, they are all about how wonderful they are and not about what they do for customers. Customer-centricity must start from right there: how you think about describing yourself to yourself and to your customers. Mission statements are also usually all about what the company does, and rarely about what they do for customers. 'We will continuously delight customers through innovative products and good quality' sounds like a customer-centred statement, but actually is not. 'To be the preferred financial services company' is not a customer-centred statement either.

Therefore, perhaps, if one were to begin at the beginning, it would be through an introspection of what the company's existence actually does for the people it sells to who generate its revenue.

We had one client in the fertilizers and pesticides business who said that he wanted to leverage his large base of customers (farmers) and diversify away from agricultural inputs because of price control, supply constraints and volatility of demand. The CEO said all he wanted was that the financial objectives be met. However, because he had no customer-based mission to go by, no 'This is what we do for customers, which makes us excited as a company' statement, and no 'This is what we do for people in our world', developing strategy was a totally confusing and, worse still, beaconless, soulless process.

CUSTOMER-BASED DASHBOARD OF ORGANIZATION PERFORMANCE

We have said right at the outset that CBBS is easier to practice if the 'where do we want to go' goals for the organization are not just defined in terms of financial metrics, but also in terms of customer-based metrics.

An extension of this is to have every critical construct and framework that strategists and the CEO in the organization talk about, in the context of their business, 'mirrored' with a customer-based metric, as illustrated in Table 10.1.

Table 10.1: Customer-Based Business Analysis		
Construct	**Inside-business view**	**Customer-based view**
Market definition	Product category	Customer need arena or value space
Market segmentation	Product segments	Customer-based segments
Growth performance	Incremental volume or value sales	Customer and consumption additions
Market growth trend analysis	What is being sold more or less and why	Increase from new consumers or existing consumers—who, where
Industry analysis	Structure of industry—conduct of players—financial performance of all players combined	Structure of customer demand—concerns and conduct of customers—satisfaction levels of all customers combined
Industry trends	Product or producer behaviour changes; segment size shifts	Customer or consumption behaviour changes, customer segments size shifts
Growth driver analysis	Macroeconomic and supply-side variables	Macro consumer and people-related variables

An even further extension of this is for every supply-side comment made during strategy meetings, one asks: 'So how would this affect customers and what would they do as a result?'

RECOGNIZING THAT EVEN A WELL-DONE BUSINESS PLAN DOES NOT CONTAIN A BUSINESS-MARKET STRATEGY

Most companies have the elaborate annual business planning ritual. It is the grand negotiation between the management and its overseeing body, usually the board, with all its constructive and destructive tension; and, finally, a set of *budget* or *target* numbers are agreed to, which in essence is a desired P&L statement, cash flow statement and capex proposals statement. Several companies do have a 'beyond the numbers' set of criteria as a part of this annual business planning cycle, like market position improvement or expansion of the scope of the business, etc. Some use a balanced score card system, which sets annual objectives not just in terms of financials, but also in terms of factors that influence the financial outcomes like customers, internal processes, learning and growth. As we said in Chapter 1, while we do sometimes see the 'customer' figure at the highest level at which business planning is done and business performance monitored, we are often disappointed with the simplistic metrics that companies choose against this bucket.

The trouble with business plans is that they go from overall targets to product-wise targets to geography-wise targets and various other sub-targets and then on to marketing action plans. But the business-market strategy is usually left undefined. The business-market strategy defines:

237

1. for the business unit as a whole,
2. what game will it play and in which parts of the market:
   (i) what rivalry proposition it will use to win the consumer and cut out the competitor, and
   (ii) how this rivalry proposition gets translated into concrete product and service offers.
3. how such a game will be supported by the rest of the organization.

Therefore, even when they copiously break down the overall target numbers into *where* the sales and profits will come from (products or product groups, geographies, customers or customer groups), and give details of all planned actions in the market, the market game that drives these actions is often not clear. The question of 'what will you do to achieve these numbers' is quite clearly answered in most business plans through what often seems to be a laundry list of initiatives that will be taken in the market or internally. However, the question of whether the actions planned are coherent with strategy or flow from a strategy is usually not answered. As we said in Chapter 2, as depicted in Figure 2.1, business planning is about implementing the chosen strategy in the market. Boards too are guilty of allowing business plans to supplant strategy, resting content if the business is meeting its numbers regularly, and seems to have a detailed set of market-place actions that help it to achieve its numbers. But do these actions and achievement of these plans make the business' market position and differentiation in the market stronger? When bad times come either on account of the environment or intensified competition, we notice that companies that have had business plans not underpinned by business-market strategy tend to get hit hard.

238

Our second *watch out* flag on conventional business planning is that it is usually very 'inside-out' and incremental, in that it starts with the current situation and asks what more or incremental can be done in the next year or few years. It does not consider the world outside, except in terms of some broad macroeconomic indicators, which are translated into broad-brush 'good times ahead or bad times ahead' signals for the incremental growth number to be pegged to. Finally, we often find that business plans go straight from *objectives* to *actions* without articulating the overall game being played in the market. This usually results in short-term solutions or diffused effort.

Not Confusing Marketing Operational Effectiveness for Business-Market Strategy

One of the most insightful articles that everyone in Indian business today, and especially in industries like IT services, must read for sure is 'What Is Strategy' by Michael E. Porter (1996). He makes the point that operational effectiveness is not strategy, and define operational effectiveness as including many practices beyond *efficiency*, which include methods to buy better, utilize its inputs better, improve time to market, etc. To that list we would like to add all more operationally efficient ways to serve customers and dealers better that often get confused as 'This is our strategy in the market'. Porter observes:

> Positioning—once the heart of strategy—is rejected as too static for today's dynamic market and changing technologies. According to the new dogma, rivals can quickly copy any market position, and competitive advantage is, at best, temporary.

But those beliefs are dangerous half-truths, and they are leading more and more companies down the path of mutually destructive competition . . .

The root of the problem is a failure to distinguish between operational effectiveness and strategy . . .

Operational effectiveness and strategy are both essential to superior performance, which, after all, is the primary goal of any enterprise. But they work in very different ways.

A company can outperform its rivals only if it can establish a difference that it can preserve. It must deliver greater value to customers or create comparable value at a lower cost, or do both. The arithmetic of superior profitability then follows: delivering greater value allows a company to charge higher average unit prices; greater efficiency results in lower average unit costs . . .

Operational effectiveness (OE) means performing similar activities *better* than how rivals perform them . . . In contrast, strategic positioning means performing activities *different* from rivals' or performing similar activities in *different* ways . . .

Constant improvement in operational effectiveness is necessary to achieve superior profitability; however, it is not usually sufficient. Few companies have competed successfully on the basis of operational effectiveness over an extended period, and staying ahead of rivals gets harder every day . . . (Porter 1996: 61–63)

MAKING THE COMMITMENT TO ADD THE 'CUSTOMER INPUT' STRAND TO THE BUSINESS STRATEGY DEVELOPMENT PROCESS THAT ALREADY EXISTS

Our book is about business strategy, which is about deciding what you want your business to achieve in a given future time frame, and figuring out how you will go about achieving it, either at an SBU level or at the overall corporate level. Several business strategy development frameworks and philosophies exist, all equally good or bad. At each step of whichever strategy development framework we use in our business, we need to ask if the customers' views and concerns have been accurately and insightfully fed in, Our mental model of how to make business strategy development more customer-based is to simply add another strong strand into the existing threads from which strategy is being woven. We do not suggest a whole new approach, but instead say that at each stage let us look at whether the inputs from the customer world and the market have been adequately taken into account.

Appendices
Articles by Rama Bijapurkar, 1998–2005

1. MANAGING THE DEMAND DIP
BusinessWorld, 22 October–6 November 1998

THE dreaded R word is everywhere. I walked into my doctor's chamber the other day and said to him, rather enviously: 'I bet you are in the one business that's recession-proof.' He shook his head sadly and said that was not strictly true, since people were 'waiting and watching' their ailments and postponing any expensive treatment that they could live without for the time being! Even my jeweller has launched simple, lighter designs, saying: 'These are times for value engineering, not value addition!' How true.

In the midst of what is being euphemistically called a 'slowdown', a 'downturn', or a 'lower than expected growth', crafting strategies to soften the inevitable blow is on top of everyone's agenda. While prescriptions for protecting the bottom line by squeezing the middle line (costs) are being rapidly put into place, the focus is *now* shifting to how best to hold the top line (revenue). There are various schools of behaviour at work here. There's the 'cut prices and grow volumes' school espoused by sections of the auto industry, the domestic airline industry's 'hike fares and grow revenues' school, Maruti Udyog's 'increase market-share by delivering superior value, not lower price' philosophy, the export market's 'let us earn in dollars rather than in rupees' policy, and as one CEO put it, the 'avoid a blunderbuss approach and choose carefully' school.

Whichever way one looks at it, the need of the hour seems to be for a special kind of strategic market management designed for coping with downturns. This would mean consciously re-thinking for the short term which customers, products and channels to serve with what intensity and how (that is, what value package of benefits and costs to offer). The caveat is that one must be able to do this so as to, figuratively speaking, temporarily disable the limbs that consume the precious oxygen without cutting off the legs altogether!

A 'bad times' strategic market management requires a special 'bad times' analysis of market structure, market segments and customer needs. Here are my suggestions on what this could entail, based on all the sound bites I have been hearing on what's happening and what needs to be done.

The prerequisite for a 'bad times analysis' is a detailed map of market structure from the customer window. For, if we do not know exactly who is buying, we cannot get to the next step: figuring out which customers get going when the going gets tough. A map from the customer window is what a lot of people do not actually have—it is not about market break-up by 'big and small refrigerators' or 'reactive and disperse dyes'. It is not even about broad-brush customer categories like 'large-city and small-town demand' or 'cotton textile mills and leather units'. It is a step more detailed. It looks at exactly which customers are buying how much of what product and at what prices.

Surprisingly, even in the fast-moving consumer goods businesses, many a time, penetration data exist for broad consumer categories, but a specific map of what percentage of total volume comes out of sharply-defined consumer segments needs to be put together. Industrial products usually do not have it, because of a tradition of selling products rather than selling to customers. Ideally, a 'good times' market structure map would be a great starting point; but then, it is better late than never to construct one even as we speak. It is money and time well worth investing.

The second step is to assess what the likely 'bad times' behaviour of each consumer segment would be, and therefore, what a 'continuing bad times' market structure could be, say, two years from now. Will corporates that buy a lot of cars continue to replace them when depreciated? Will self-employed professionals do the same? I just heard a brown goods category manager say: 'If the situation gets worse, the higher-priced replacement market (in metros) will account for a much higher proportion of the total market five years hence; we aren't ready for that today, because we have been focusing on first-time buyers, at the lower-priced and small-town end of the market, who have been traditionally fuelling growth.' A pharmaceutical industry guru said in a recent speech that he felt 'older medicines, tonics and such discretionary purchases will decline, while life-saving drugs will continue to grow' (at the expense of some other non-pharma category perhaps?). Obviously, this analysis will be hard to do, if all we have to go by is that sluggish gross domestic product growth has slowed down refrigerator growth, or that a wayward index of industrial production has caused havoc with demand for chain-pulley blocks.

An even better thing to do would be to re-segment the customer base along dimensions that affect behaviour during bad times, and do a 'what if' analysis of each such segment. I once did some work for a packaging product, and the managing director of the company said that the market size forecasts were overly bullish. 'What happens if the bottom falls out of exports of gems and jewellery, or if state governments, in their quest for revenue, change the duty structure for liquor, making premium brands out-priced'? The segmentation he was asking for was: a break-up of the tonnage of his products by likely behaviour of his customers and likely stability of their markets (for example, judging the pros and cons of proactively cutting packaging costs at the first sign of trouble versus hanging in there until pushed to a wall) and within each of those segments, which are stable end-use markets and which unstable.

Diagnose the cause of demand slowdown for your business—it may be surmountable. People do have money. The savings rate is going up, but people are not spending, not because they do not have the money but because consumer confidence is low. People believe that tomorrow will be worse than today, and that it's time to not be wasteful or indulgent. So, is your product being promoted as a utility or a luxury item? Is there another way of getting consumers to process price? Are there parts of the utility market that you can go after aggressively? Perhaps the gift market, linked to a public face, is less vulnerable for the same category, than the personal use market?

If you are in an industrial market, selling intermediate products to customers who in turn serve end consumers, the push to hold on to the customer from the predatory price-slashing competitor is very real. This is the time to bond with the troubled customer, but in a manner that does not drain your bottom line. An analysis of the reasons for your customers' demand slowdown and their responses to it will help select the good guys to partner. This is exactly like evaluating marriage proposals—not everyone is good marriage material. The purpose of a partnership is to create and share the fruits of work jointly in, say, logistics and usage of your products, or in joint product development to deliver better value to the end customer. Examples of the former are several in India. A perfume company servicing a personal products giant decided that instead of taking yet another beating on price, it would collaborate to change the stage in the manufacturing process where its perfume was used, and that the 'evaporation' savings would be jointly shared. A bulk chemical company decided to save on transport costs by transporting in detachable balloons rather than by tankers and to share the saving on the return transport cost of the empty tanker.

And finally, a corollary to deciding whom to partner is: whom to dump? We need to do some sensitive analysis to identify certain customer segments which provide too much pain and too little gain. In good times, they may offer certain strategic or financial value, but in bad times, are just not worth bothering about. In other words, who cares about the icing, if the entire cake is going bad? A 'volume builder' segment that provides perceived image-building market muscle may not be as necessary to serve in bad times as one that provides real trade clout or keeps capacity utilization up and hence keeps costs in certain other segments down.

That's it for this column—my prescription of the 'R' spectacles through which to look at recessionary markets, and rethink strategies for staying afloat.

2. CULTURAL LABELS

Business World, 14–20 June 1999

MY daughter and I had yet another argument over the cellphone. She wanted to borrow it when she was on the move, working on a school project, and I was horrified. 'If you can say yes without a fuss to the laptop why not the cellphone?' she asked. The answer of course was that in her mind, they were both productivity devices, while in my mind, one was a necessary academic tool while the other was a luxury, a needless indulgence, which she ought not to have, unless she earned it herself. My mother, at 69, struggles to get Internet literate (she has never used a computer in her life), and asks if we can help her buy a cheap computer. She refuses to get herself a decent air-conditioner, despite the scorching Hyderabad summer, saying that she is a simple soul, with simple habits. She sees the computer as a 'family bonding' device that enables her to do her job as family matriarch better. However, she sees the air-conditioner as the symbol of the new materialistic culture that she is constantly warning us to protect our children from!

Recently, I re-read a fifties' piece of work by Ernest Dichter, the father of motivation research, applied to marketing. This was about a study that he did in order to develop a strategy to increase coffee consumption in America. One of the first questions that he asked and set out to answer was: 'What is coffee's cultural label? What should be coffee's cultural status in the future?' The concept of the cultural label of a product category has always fascinated me—it sets the boundaries of consumer demand, determines 'what business are you in', hones in on which other categories you are competing with, and determines what dimensions consumers use when processing value delivered by you. Remember the cultural label of the watch category in India before Titan? It was clearly seen as a utilitarian timekeeping device, offered by a company whose self-image was that of being 'timekeepers to the nation'. Over time, courtesy Titan, it moved on to become a lower order personal apparel accessory (like a belt or shoes), and is now spreading to also occupy the same cultural label as jewellery and haute couture fashion accessories. Needless to say, changes in the cultural label of the category—the way it is perceived and the way it is seen fitting into the lives of people—changes a lot of things for the marketer.

Back to Dichter's analysis. He concluded that what was limiting consumption of coffee was that it had become a utilitarian staple, and that it must be rediscovered as an exciting beverage of pleasure. His recommendations were 'change coffee from a sinful and escapist beverage (hazardous to health, promoted addiction and an aid to laziness) to a positive life-accepting product, a food for emotional health (a symbol of sociability and hospitality, an evoker of nostalgic feeling about childhood pleasures and security, a symbol of grown-up relaxation.)' He also felt that coffee should catch up with the cultural changes that were happening in America at that time, represented by a desire for more gracious living, the moving away from earlier restrictions on sensory pleasures and the trend towards expression of personality by more individualized consumption and enjoyment of differences and variety.

The point about how categories must be made to catch up with cultural changes in their consumer's lives is particularly relevant for us. Culturally, many things have changed. But some categories are still 'frozen psychologically', because marketers are afraid to make the change and help the category catch up with the cultural change in its consumers' lives. Take bicycles. Or decorative wall paints. Or bedsheets. In some cases the categories have evolved culturally but the marketers are frozen in time.

Colour cosmetics are changing their cultural label from 'enticement aid', which 'nice girls don't', to 'grooming' amongst older women, and 'self-expression of individuality' among the young ones. Akai proclaims that it has changed the cultural label of TVs (among lower-end buyers) from a statement of lifestyle to a 'utility, just like a tap'. Of course taps are trying to change their label from a utility to a statement of lifestyle!

Cultural labels get formed in different ways— communication from marketers to buyers (a lot of cellphone communication tells me that it is for husbands who ring their wives and say 'I'll be home in 15 minutes', and young women who invite their boyfriends to dinner at restaurants!); from the way media and film portray the category (why does the villain and not the hero wear dark glasses?); by the way people use the category, in the context of their lives. Cultural labels are not static—they change with the changing discourse in the world around the category.

Tailpiece: In the Indian cultural context, machines are 'master', while in the West, they are 'servant'. (For those who disagree, think about what we do to all our gadgets on Dussehra/Ayudha puja day!) Does this explain some of the mystique in consumer decision making on durables?

3. MONEY MOTIVES

Business World, 19 July 1999

I HAVE for some time had the sneaking suspicion that Mars and Venus is not just about the gender divide but about the finance-marketing divide as well. Fifteen years ago, I had a hardcore finance person as my boss, and our conversations usually ended with his shaking his head in bewilderment and saying, in his inimitable Bengali accent: 'I will nevher understand the covher and com-meet philosophy of you marketing types.'

'You all commit first and then try to cover, while we cover first and then commit,' he would say, in aggrieved response to my insistence that a huge amount of money needed to be spent on advertising first, before any sales would be forthcoming.

More recently, after I moved into my new office, marketing friends who visited me would approvingly say: 'Great office; of course, you could manage with less, but then it's bad for your brand.' My ever rational finance friends would inevitably say: 'You don't need this much space for a man and dog operation. If you consider the interest cost of advance rent and look at the return on capital employed, you will be more gainfully employed supervising homework and attending PTA meetings.'

And herein lies the Mars-Venus divide. To them, money is money, but to me, money is a means to enhancing my identity and self-worth. And that is the reason I would be a sitting duck for someone who creates 'Stree Shakti' bonds, and promises that a part of the money raised will be loaned to women entrepreneurs. I can almost hear the rational Martian asking:

'Would you still invest in that, if the yield was lower than what others are offering?' And my answer would be that I would add emotional benefits yielded to the yield calculation, and decide.

This does, however, upset the fervently held belief on Mars that customers look at only three criteria when making investment decisions—risk, return and liquidity—and that the world of customers and their investment behaviour can neatly be segmented into combinations of risk-return-liquidity levels desired, all calculable by even the most mediocre mind. Are all marital fights about money merely because high liquidity is married to high return? Or is there something more fundamental going on there?

There is, and I read about it with fascination, in an article by Diana Wright in the *Sunday Times* (reproduced in *The Times of India*). Wright tells of the work of Adrian Furnham, professor of psychology at University College, London, and joint author of *The Psychology of Money*, who makes a compelling case that 'our attitudes to money are strongly linked to our emotions. Four basic emotions are most commonly singled out as underpinning our attitudes to money. Our desires for security, love, power and freedom dictate different ways in which we use our money'.

The article talks of many interesting segments. There is the security seeker, 'who is a compulsive saver and hoarder and for whom saving is its own reward'. Not much joy there for credit cards, but a bank's customer base made up of these would be great—keep cross-selling and locking him up further. Then, there is another type of security seeker, a 'compulsive bargain hunter, who fanatically holds on to his cash, until he finds the perfect deal. For him, the thrill is in outsmarting others rather than in acquiring something he wants'. Here is the perfect customer for a complicated investment option, where the joy is in discovering how exactly the calculation works. Count me out on this one!

The next type is the power broker who sees 'money as a means of power/importance/dominance/control'. Different descriptors have been used for them, two of them being 'empire builders', and 'Godfather type, using money principally to control others'. I now know why my uncle used to have his meagre money in a wide array of investments, with complicated nominations. He would have instantly defected to a bank that offered him a 'joint' account with his spouse, with several conditions on how and where and when she could withdraw the money.

Then there is the love dealer who sees money as a means to buy love, affection and a sense of self-worth. They are divided into the love buyers and the love sellers— love buyers are those who 'purchase love with generous presents—which may also include making ostentatious gifts to charity'. So those who created the credit cards where a percentage of the bill goes to charity could also have a more profitable version, where the card holder pays for that donation to charity! And, of course, it's nice to know that the gift market for money is alive and well, but take care: the investment products that the love dealer and the power broker may want to gift would be completely different!

And finally, there is the freedom seeker, for whom money is a symbol of independence, 'which they value more than love'. So maybe there is not just the worried 'about to be pensioned' old man, but the 'I want to be free at last' young man, who is ready to save for his pension, in the prime of his burdened youth!

4 BUSINESS UNUSUAL

Business World, 22 October 2001

ANALYSES of corporate results of 2000–01 and Q1 2001–02 give cause for concern. Topline growth has been much slower than bottomline growth, which, in turn, has been achieved not from improved operating profit margins, but from lower costs and higher other income. (*Economic Times Survey* 2000-01: top-line growth of 17.6per cent, operating profit margin slightly down, net profit growth of 37 per cent. *Business Standard Survey* Q1 2001–02 vs previous year: sales growth of 5.3 per cent, unchanged operating profit margins, net profit growth of 12.7 per cent.) Even for very smart companies, it will be hard to replicate the early wins of such a strategy in subsequent quarters. Aggressive cost cutting can help to an extent, but such aggression, beyond a point, could result in cutting not just fat, but muscle as well, leading to the vicious cycle of short-term results at the expense of long-term competitiveness.

The biggest challenge before companies is to grow the topline in a slow economy—to swim against a receding tide. The disturbing pattern that emerges from company after company that I talk to is that top management's first initiative towards growing the topline is to flog the marketing and sales departments, and tell them to go into a frenzy in their rain dance and make rain happen. They, in turn, chase hard to reach targets, through the potent compound of high aggression diligence: a large part of it involves leaning on the trade and offering price discounts and freebies to buy the customer. This ends in the pyrrhic victory—the targets are met, but at a cost higher than usual, and with no guarantees of what will happen the next quarter, when the incentives are withdrawn. In fact, we have already seen the cycle of 'upstocking the trade' in previous quarters being followed by the cycle of slower primary sales and faster retail sales. The message is: As you sow, so shall you reap!

How much longer can growth be driven this way, given today's situation of increasingly exhausted marketing and sales departments, rebellious trade, and a bargain-hunting, procrastinating customer?

It is time to tackle this problem at the level of the business or business unit as a whole. Producing growth in tough times requires far more than a collection of individuals working in overdrive in one functional area, trying every trick in the marketing textbook to maximize the sales of their individual products or brands. It is time for more than push-harder-in-business-as-usual. It is time for senior management to engage in a formal and disciplined process of developing a market strategy for the business as a whole and spell out (i) which parts of the market the business will focus on, and with what intensity, to make this growth happen; and (ii) what the business will offer to customers in each part of the market, to get them to make the buy-me decision. It requires senior management to sit down and undertake tie following:

- Adopt a realistic and shared view of what is going on in the market and why and where it is headed (arrived at from a bottom-up analysis and understanding of customer types and their behaviour, not product types and their sales trends). This will suggest the choice of growth routes to take, and determine the degree by which the conventional business boundaries and rules of the game can be stretched.
- Identify all possible routes to growth and understand what needs to be done to succeed on each route. These must range from what we may call 'business as usual' to 'business unusual'—a lovely phrase that I borrow from a television programme by Andersen Consulting (now Accenture). It immediately means doing things that 'we have never done before', or which 'is not the norm in our industry'. One example of this is 'Redefining business boundaries'—why not trade in second-hand cars, why

not hire out motorcycles, why not source and distribute Chinese competition products proactively? The other example is to have innovative value propositions for the customer. Why not offer a range of hotels for 'sensible', 'modern', senior corporate executives that is low on price, high on status and business facilities and low on social amenities? Why not re-segment the market along new benefit dimensions and create new categories? Why not SMS-only services for teenagers, and so on?

- Make choices and establish clear priorities: decide which of these growth routes the organization must pursue with what intensity (depending on gain and pain plus risk that each involves—pain and risk being determined by an understanding of what needs to be done and spent in order to succeed on a given route).

- Develop further, for each chosen route, consumer offers and business systems to deliver these propositions. (What exactly will this high-status, low-price hotel have? How do you deliver this profitably?)

The process is simple and rather obvious. But for something really useful to come out of it, there has to be a huge commitment to do this in an 'outside-in' manner. This is a big move away from the typical 'inside-out' approach, which starts with the question, 'Which parts of my business should I push harder?' The 'inside-out' approach often ends up in a decision to push high-margin products, or historically good-growth product segments, whereas the drivers of future growth could lie somewhere else. Maybe where the company is not even present. In contrast, the 'outside-in' approach starts with a detailed map of the market out there and asks, 'Which parts of our business should we be entering or pushing harder?' (Breakthrough growth routes are found only if this map is comprehensive and customer-centric. 'Comprehensive' means it does not leave out any market space where the customer is spending money for this need—including the grey market, the unorganized sector, home-grown solutions, money spent on services required to use the product, and so on. 'Customer-centric' means that the map starts with customer types and what they want and, thus, what they buy, rather than product types alone.)

Let me share my checklist. With it, one can scrutinize the market map and identify growth options:

BUSINESS AS USUAL

- Growth opportunities resulting from working harder and better at 'business as usual': Is there scope for existing brands/products/services to improve their customer-perceived value via a relaunch/ re-stage or any customer-focused activity?
- Is there scope for fill-in-the-blanks growth? That is, from entering product-markets/consumer segment/ distribution channel/geographic spaces where you are not present, or are weak and which you have ignored as 'historical weakness', or not-quite-our-area-of-strength product?
- Is there scope for growth by increasing market share through marketing operational performance improvement initiatives? Example: any CRM activity, actually resulting in improved service levels (there is still lots of room for that), doing better (more customer empathetic) advertising?
- Is there scope for growth from using the distribution channel more innovatively? Example: converting

dealers of intermediate products with a fragmented customer base into solution sellers, rather than mere product suppliers (as in the case of say polyurethane for cold storages, small footwear factories, construction applications, etc.). Example: 'rewriting the contract' with dealers, making them offer more customer services and capturing a larger share of customer spend?

- Is there scope for launching a new brand in an existing market space, where the company is unrepresented, or where the competitor brand is jaded and floundering?

OPPORTUNITIES OF BUSINESS AS USUAL

- Growth opportunities resulting from working smarter at 'business as usual': Is there competitor share to be gained from smart re-segmenting of the market along new dimensions, like customer types with distinctive needs or usage benefits (instead of product attributes) and creating a new set of offers (which could be modified versions of your existing offers?). Many markers are still product segmented and there is a possibility of huge customer-perceived value by being the first to do it.
- If you are the category leader and the category is not growing, rather than wait for growth, you need to put the magic back into the category, rekindle interest in it and, thereby, activate the desire to buy/replace.
- Are there new category values that can be created to make the category grow? Should a category be divided into sub-categories with different values to capture more growth? Example: cell phones with category values of safety, rather than indulgence or convenience devices for women and children; vehicles which are work partners,

rather than personal transportation; cooking appliances which offer health and nutrition benefits.

OPPORTUNITIES OF BUSINESS UNUSUAL

- Redefining business boundaries: Which are the related market spaces in which you could compete, but are not doing so because of historical definitions of business scope? Example: repair and maintenance services, second-hand vehicle buyers, product use training, any other products or services that the customer needs in order to use your products, as with paints. Any other product/ services used in addition to or instead of your products.

- Market creation: Creating new price performance points backed by appropriate business models to capture new high-volume opportunities. (Example: Nirma, Suvidha of Citibank, Subhiksha, bridging the gap between bicycles and mopeds to help bicycle users upgrade, better power tillers for the small farmer, finding propositions backed by business models that can satisfy the need of low income customers for telephone access, without requiring a minimum expenditure per line to make it profitable for the company, smaller, cheaper air-conditioners that cool without chilling you to the bones.)

- Enabling people with the desire but not the ability to afford consumer products at existing price points through innovation in pricing and new paradigms for buying or using. (Example: life-time maintenance contracts, community use ISD/STD booths, cybercafes, rental of Polaroid cameras and two wheelers.)

- Creating new performance categories in the market to serve poorly fulfilled needs. (Example: Maxidor three-wheelers for short distance rural transport, small tractors reconfigured to small earth-moving equipment.)

- Breaking category norms and gaining share. Every category has several unwritten rules in crafting offers to consumers, which the consumer has been taught to believe. Cultural analysts call these the 'category codes' (or 'doesn't everyone know'). Big cars are more prestigious than small ones. Big size refrigerators have more advanced features than small ones. 150cc is a racing bike, 100cc is a roadster. High-tech is used to serve rich customers, since poor customers are not tech-happy. Five-star hotels are high on status while three-stars are not. Most of them have no real basis to be true, but are adhered to. Is there opportunity to grow by breaking these codes? The Boston Consulting Group has published a very interesting book, called *Breaking Compromises*, which is about growing through breaking the compromises that industries have made consumers accept as a 'fact of life'.

- A popularly used growth option killer is this: 'We cannot compete profitably here; our cost base/business model does not permit it; this is not our market.' The question from the perspective of growth is this: Are you looking for only that growth which your existing business model can deliver? (Chances are that in the past few years you have squeezed out a lot of it.) Or are you willing to look at all possible growth avenues, and see if you can find a business model that gives them what they need, and do so profitably?

POSTSCRIPT

I am often told that talking about the economic slowdown and the advent of a tougher phase II of demand is alarmist.

It gives the troops a chance to say: 'Can't be done!' But I am at a loss to understand how any carrot-and-stick ploy can make an auto component maker for, say, trucks, achieve 30 per cent-plus profitable growth this year, when fewer new trucks are being sold and existing trucks are not working hard enough to wear out their components faster.

You can continue with the 'work harder at business as usual' form of swimming against the tide, if you believe (a) that the tide has not receded too far and (b) that this is just a temporary blip and, if we hang in there, very soon natural growth and buoyancy will return to the market. How far out the tide is today depends on which set of numbers you believe in. (An article I read recently pointed out that there are three official figures for last year's GDP growth: 6.5 per cent, 6.0 per cent and 5.2 per cent.) It also depends on what your perspective is on the 'realness' of services sector growth—its composition and ability to drive consumer demand. From all the economist-speak I have read, the tide is expected to turn sometime in the last quarter of this year. But the consensus on that seems to be that when the tide does indeed turn, it will be a slow tide.

5. LOW PRICE. WHAT PERFORMANCE?

BusinessWorld, 13 June 2005

THANK god for C.K. Prahalad. But for him, a simple truth would not have been acknowledged in boardrooms around the world: that people with less money desire all the same things that people with more money do, but do not buy them because they cannot afford to. And growth strategies would not have concerned themselves with the idea of a price-performance point (as opposed to just a price point), which enables both consumer happiness and business profitability. To use a CK-ism, we would still have been trapped in the 'tyranny of OR'. Customer happiness OR business profitability. High price OR high profits.

The arithmetic of consumer demand in a country as poor as ours is very clear. At lower prices, there will be a lot of people consuming a little bit each, which can add up to a lot. Businesses in the telecom and FMCG sectors have already proven this.

However, there are two big challenges in tapping the demand potential that modest-income consumers offer. One, given the price that they can afford, the challenge is to determine the right configuration of performance ('What benefit bundle to offer?') that maximizes value to customers and minimizes cost to the company. There is little room for manoeuvre in the price the consumer can afford. The second challenge centres around how to drive production, delivery and marketing costs down to maximize profit for the chosen benefit bundle.

This column is about finding the right performance configuration or benefit bundle. I would include innovative pricing, credit, economy in use, method of purchase, after sales care, etc., in the benefit bundle. It is, in consumer speak, 'what I give', 'what I get' and 'what I give up'. Everyone is familiar with the design principle of creating a low-priced offering: provide minimum acceptable functionality and cut out the frills. However, the consumer is the only arbiter of what 'minimum acceptable' functionality is, and what an unwanted frill is. Companies often forget this, and design the offering based on 'what manufacturers think'!

Hindustan Lever decided to drive the low price/discount/ popular market. But in an attempt to better margins, they slowly brought down product quality (e.g. TFM in soaps).

This made their brands very vulnerable, even to competition whose performance was marginally better at a given price point.

Moped makers offered sub-optimal performance at a low price, and as soon as better options were available, consumers rushed to deferred purchase or second-hand motorcycles. Clearly, the price point was OK; the performance point was not.

I think Big Bazaar and Subhiksha have got the price-performance equation right. The early wave of modern retailers added cost to themselves, but not much value to customers to justify that cost. So they got relegated to 'indulgence/feel-good/special items' shopping—a small and dispensable part of the total shopping basket. My Reliance cellphone had a great price-performance equation. However, the 'Hindi only'-speaking customer care people, while costing Reliance less, caused me more stress as a customer.

I am personally delighted with the idea of a 'low price' hotel chain that offers adequate performance on quality of room, amenities, service, location and status cues. For years, I have struggled with having to choose between a decent hotel at ridiculously high prices and crummy hotels which are affordable but where I cannot stay. There has not been a middle segment. The inns, lodges, 3-stars and guesthouses have poor performance points: dirty sheets and bathrooms, sleazy waiters, terrible service and poor communication facilities.

The question is: what is the right benefit bundle for a low cost? What do you want me to sacrifice for the lower price that I pay? No room service? Fine, I can live with it. A coffee and tea vending machine and a water cooler, conveniently located on my floor, are infinitely preferable to sleazy low-wage waiters, speaking in any language. But if the unintended consequence of it is that I have to begin my day running into a lot of men in their *lungis* and bare torsos getting their morning cuppa or night bottle of water, I think it is a huge price to pay. This cannot be a place where families and women stay.

I am, however, willing to give up flowers and pretty paintings in the room, cardboard wrappers for toiletries or even toiletries themselves. But stained sheets and harsh towels? No. Good quality sheets and towels not changed every day? Yes. There is an implicit programming in my head of what is functionality and what are frills. Different segments of consumers will have different programming on this. And there is, I am sure, a clear cost analysis in the head of the marketer of what adds to the cost and what does not, what is sustainable and what is not. The trick is to match the two for a segment that is large enough and clearly defined.

The consumer part is harder and more painstaking. Most people use the complicated technical way, that is, to make a laundry list of features they plan or do not plan to. They then do lots of conjoint analyses and concept tests to measure consumer trade-offs. However, creative solutions to manage the tricky equation of minimizing cost to the company and maximizing value perceived by customers will not emerge from here. The smarter, though harder, approach is to do some good quality, open-minded consumer listening to understand the consumer's 'need logic' and 'need drivers'.

The following points help in that process. The context in which a consumer uses the product—I use a hotel to sleep in and prepare for my meetings, for my private face and not my public one. The value space in the consumer's head where the product resides—for me, a hotel is about enabling my productivity and not sending out negative status signals. The benefit structure logic—home-like physical comfort, preserving physical and psychological energy, quality amenities at a fee, making me feel safe and contributing to psychological comfort. How prices are processed in the head—I do not mind paying a steep rate for a business centre service, but I do mind paying an arm and a leg for my tea.

Based on this consumer logic, the configuration of performance can be designed, and tested against the need hierarchy of consumers. What do they feel are the table stakes, without which they will not even play? What are the dissatisfiers, things without which the consumer feels unhappy? What are the value adders? What are the balance tillers?

The visiting head of R&D for a medical systems company asked: 'But if I need to give good quality diagnostics for everyone, whether rich or poor, how can I lower performance points and do a stripped down version?' The question is a fair one. And the answer lies in understanding clearly that the core functionality of the product and service cannot be compromised at any price point, but frills can.

The readings of the diagnostic machine and promptly fixing the breakdowns are non-negotiable. The rest of it is negotiable. Outright purchase versus hire or pay as you use is negotiable. Keeping records in the memory of the machine or in a printed file is negotiable. Perhaps. If we understand the customer value processing logic and the context of usage very well, more innovative designs are likely to emerge.

Bibliography

Aaker, David A. 1998. *Developing Business Strategies*, 5th edition. New York: John Wiley & Sons.

Christenson, Clayton M. 1997. *The Innovator's Dilemma—When New Technologies Cause Great Firms to Fail*. Boston, MA: Harvard Business School Press.

Coyne, Kevin P. and Somu Subramaniam. 1996. 'Bringing Discipline to Strategy', *McKinsey Quarterly*, Number 4, pp. 61–70. Available online at http://www. global50discoveries. com/LinkClick.aspx?fileticket=X_J9xwHg9WU%3D&ta bid=396&mid=1185

Day, George S. 1990. *Market Driven Strategy: Processes for Creating Value*. New York: The Free Press.

Dwight L. Gertz and Joao P.A. Baptista. 1995. *Grow To Be Great—Breaking the Downsizing Cycle*. New York: The Free Press.

Hamel, Gary. 1996. 'Strategy as Revolution', *Harvard Business Review*, 74(4, July): 69–82.

———. 2002. *Leading the Revolution*, revised edition. Boston, MA: Harvard Business School Press.

Hamel, Gary and C.K. Prahalad. 1996. *Competing for the Future*. Boston, MA: Harvard Business School Press.

Harvard Business Essentials: Strategy. 2005. Boston, MA: Harvard Business School Press, Harvard Business Essentials.

Hax, Arnoldo and Nicholas Majluf. 1995. *The Strategy Concept and Process: A Pragmatic Approach*, 2nd edition. Upper Saddle River, NJ: Prentice-Hall.

Kim, W. Chan and Reneé Mauborgne. 2005. *Blue Ocean Strategy: How to Create Uncontested Market Space and*

Make Competition Irrelevant. Boston, MA: Harvard Business School Press.

Lanning, Michael J. 2000. *Delivering Profitable Value: A Revolutionary Framework to Accelerate Growth, Generate Wealth and Rediscover the Heart of Business*, new edition. New York, NY: Perseus Publishing.

Levitt, Theodore. 2006. *Ted Levitt on Marketing*. Boston, MA: Harvard Business School Publishing Corp.

MacMillan, I.C. 1982. 'Seizing Competitive Initiative', *The Journal of Business Strategy*, 2(4, Spring): 43–57.

McGovern, Gail, David Court, John A. Quelch, and Blair Crawford. 2004. 'Bringing Customers into the Boardroom', *Harvard Business Review*, 82(11, November): 70–80.

McKinsey & Company. 2007. 'The Bird of Gold: The Rise of India's Consumer Market', May. Available online at http://www.mckinsey.com/mgi/publica-tions/India_consumer_market/index.asp

Mintzberg, Henry, Bruce Ahlstrand, and Joseph Lamper. 1998. *Strategy Safari: A Guided Tour through the Wilds of Strategic Management*. New York: The Free Press.

Mittal, Banwari and Jagdish N. Sheth. 2001. *Value Space: Winning the Battle for Market Leadership*. New York: McGraw-Hill.

Montgomery, Cynthia A. and Michael E. Porter. 1990. *Strategy: Seeking and Securing Competitive Advantage*. New York: McGraw-Hill.

Myers, James H. 1976. 'Benefit Structure Analysis: A New Tool for Product Planning', *Journal of Marketing*, 40(October): 23–32.

Ohmae, Kenichi. 1988. 'Getting Back to Strategy', *Harvard Business Review*, 66(November): 149–56.

———. 1991. *The Mind of the Strategist: The Art of Japanese Business*. New York: McGraw-Hill.

———. 1999. *The Borderless World: Power and Strategy in the Interlinked Economy*, revised edition. New York: Harper Business.

Porter, Michael E. 1980. *Competitive Strategy*. New York: The Free Press.

————. 1982. *Cases in Competitive Strategy*. New York: The Free Press.

————. 1985. *Competitive Advantage*. New York: The Free Press.

————. 1996. 'What is Strategy', *Harvard Business Review*, (November–December): 61–78. Available online at http://www.ipocongress.ru/download/guide/article/what_is_strategy.pdf

Prahalad, C.K. and Venkat Ramaswamy. 2004. *The Future of Competition: Co-creating Unique Value with Customers*. Boston, MA: Harvard Business School Press.

Ramchander, S. 2002. *Ascending the Value Spiral*. New Delhi: SAGE Response.

Silverstein, Michael J. and George Stalk. 2000. *Breaking Compromises—Opportunities for Action in Consumer Markets from the Boston Consulting Group*. New York: John Wiley & Sons.

Wind, Yoram and Thomas S. Robertson. 1983. 'Marketing Strategy: New Directions for Theory and Research', *Journal of Marketing*, 47(Spring): 12–25.